GOOD NIGHT MRS PUFFIN

A Play in Three Acts

by

ARTHUR LOVEGROVE

SAMUEL FRENCH

LONDON
NEW YORK   TORONTO   SYDNEY   HOLLYWOOD

Copyright © 1963 Arthur Lovegrove
All Rights Reserved

GOOD NIGHT MRS PUFFIN is fully protected under the copyright laws of the British Commonwealth, including Canada, the United States of America, and all other countries of the Copyright Union. All rights, including professional and amateur stage productions, recitation, lecturing, public reading, motion picture, radio broadcasting, television and the rights of translation into foreign languages are strictly reserved.

ISBN 978-0-573-01163-4

www.samuelfrench.co.uk
www.samuelfrench.com

FOR AMATEUR PRODUCTION ENQUIRIES

UNITED KINGDOM AND WORLD EXCLUDING NORTH AMERICA

plays@SamuelFrench-London.co.uk

020 7255 4302/01

Each title is subject to availability from Samuel French,

depending upon country of performance.

CAUTION: Professional and amateur producers are hereby warned that *GOOD NIGHT MRS PUFFIN* is subject to a licensing fee. Publication of this play does not imply availability for performance. Both amateurs and professionals considering a production are strongly advised to apply to the appropriate agent before starting rehearsals, advertising, or booking a theatre. A licensing fee must be paid whether the title is presented for charity or gain and whether or not admission is charged.

The professional rights in this play are controlled by Samuel French Ltd, 52 Fitzroy Street, London, W1T 5JR

No one shall make any changes in this title for the purpose of production. No part of this book may be reproduced, stored in a retrieval system, or transmitted in any form, by any means, now known or yet to be invented, including mechanical, electronic, photocopying, recording, videotaping, or otherwise, without the prior written permission of the publisher. No one shall upload this title, or part of this title, to any social media websites.

The right of Arthur Lovegrove to be identified as author of this work has been asserted in accordance with Section 77 of the Copyright, Designs and Patents Act 1988.

GOOD NIGHT MRS PUFFIN

Produced by James P. Sherwood at the Strand Theatre, London, on the 18th July, 1961, and subsequently at the Duchess Theatre, London, with the following cast of characters —

(in the order of their appearance)

Ethel Fordyce	Cicely Hullett
Jacqueline Fordyce	Margo Mayne
Pamela Fordyce	Jill Hyem
Nicholas Fordyce	Rodney Diak
Annie	Barbara Whatley
Amelia Puffin	Irene Handl
Henry Fordyce	Jack Allen
Stephen Parker	Keneth Thornett
Victor Parker	Brian Parker
Roger Vincent	Murray Kash

Directed by Alexander Dore

Decor by John Piper

SYNOPSIS OF SCENES

The action of the Play passes in the drawing-room of the Fordyce family at their house in Hampstead

ACT I

A week before Christmas. About 4 p.m.

ACT II

Later that evening

ACT III

Three days later. Evening.

During Act III the lights are lowered for a few moments to denote the passage of one hour

Time—the present

GOOD NIGHT MRS PUFFIN

ACT I

SCENE—*The drawing-room of the Fordyce family at their house in Hampstead. A week before Christmas. About 4 p.m.*
It is a nicely furnished room that has the air of being lived-in. Double doors C *of the back wall, approached by two steps, lead to the hall and other parts of the house off* L. *A door down* R *leads to the study. A bay window* R *overlooks the garden, with the bare branches of the trees and houses in the distance. The fireplace is* L. *There are built-in shelves filling the back wall,* R *and* L *of the double doors. A long table stands in the window bay, with a Christmas tree and Christmas cards on it. A smaller table, on which there is a large table-lamp and a telephone, stands in the corner up* R. *A small console for drinks is under the shelves up* L. *Above the fireplace there is a television set on which stands a table-lamp. A large sofa is* RC *with easy chairs to match up* LC *and down* L. *A low coffee-table is in front of the sofa. The shelves up* R *carry books, ornaments and Christmas cards. The shelves up* L *have ornaments, Christmas cards and various bottles of drinks on the bottom shelf. There are more Christmas cards on the mantelpiece along with an ornate gilt clock. A good picture, in a heavy frame, hangs over the fireplace. There are electric wall-brackets over the fireplace, with the switches* R *of the doors up* C. *A small occasional table stands down* L *of the easy chair* LC. *Against the back wall of the hall is a console table with a bowl of flowers, and above it, an electric wall-bracket. The window has heavy curtains and pelmet.*
When the CURTAIN *rises, it is about 4 p.m. The light is beginning to fade and the room is brightened by the glow from the fire.* ETHEL FORDYCE *is seated on the sofa, opening letters from a pile on the coffee-table in front of her. She is aged about fifty, plump and rather fussy. She opens a letter and reads it aloud.*

ETHEL (*reading*) "Mr and Mrs Hicks thank Mr and Mrs Fordyce for their kind invitation to the wedding of their daughter Jacqueline on December the twenty-sixth, which they have much pleasure in accepting". They would! (*She picks up another, opens it and reads*) "Sir William and Lady Francis . . ." (*She mumbles away to herself and finishes triumphantly*) ". . . and have much pleasure in accepting". Oh, I am glad! (*And very obviously she is*)

(JACQUELINE *and* PAMELA FORDYCE *enter up* C. JACKY *is aged about twenty-three and is very attractive.* PAMELA *is aged about twenty and is pleasant rather than pretty. They wear outdoor clothes and are both loaded with parcels*)

PAMELA }
JACKY } (*as they enter; together*) Hallo, Mummy darling!
ETHEL. Hallo, darlings, you're back.

(JACKY *kisses Ethel, drops her parcels on the floor down* LC, *kneels and sorts them*)

JACKY. Tea ready, yet? I'm absolutely dying for a cup.

(PAMELA *moves to the fireplace, drops her parcels on the hearth-rug, kneels and sorts them*)

PAMELA. So am I. Isn't Christmas shopping sheer hell!
ETHEL. You will have to wait. Annie's busy and so am I.
PAMELA (*rising and running to Ethel*) Oh, Mummy, more acceptances and regrets? (*She sits* L *of Ethel on the sofa*)
ETHEL. The usual acceptances from those we don't want and regrets from those we do. (*She reads another letter*) "Mr and Mrs Higglethorpe . . ." Higglethorpe—who on earth are they? We don't know anyone of that name.
JACKY. Higglethorpe? Oh, they're cousins of Victor, once or twice removed.
PAMELA. I bet they are coming.
ETHEL. Oh, they are. And we've had an acceptance from Sir William and Lady Francis. Isn't that nice?
JACKY. Why? We don't know them.
ETHEL. No, but we will.
PAMELA (*rising*) Of course. (*She removes her coat and throws it over the back of the easy chair* LC) People can hardly come to the wedding without meeting the bride's mother. (*She collects her parcels, crosses and puts them on the table* R)
ETHEL. Well, it's very nice to meet people. (*She opens another letter*)
PAMELA. Oh, Mummy. (*She crosses and kneels on the hearth-rug*)
ETHEL (*reading the letter*) Oh, your Aunt Alice is coming. (*She is not too happy about this*)
JACKY. Not with our ghastly cousin Hector?
ETHEL. That's no way to speak of your cousin. I cannot imagine why you didn't have him as a page boy. I always think a page in white satin gives tone.

(JACKY *rises, collects her parcels and puts them on the table* R)

JACKY. You could dress Hector in royal purple and he'd still look ghastly.
ETHEL (*opening another letter*) That's most unkind. (*She reads the letter*) There, I knew it! Aunt Vera has accepted and wants to know why the wedding is so rushed. Reading between the lines . . .
JACKY (*leaning over the back of the sofa,* L *of Ethel*) Aunt Vera has a dirty mind.

ETHEL. Darling, I wouldn't say that, but I do hope you don't have a baby too soon. People talk so. Look at poor Cynthia. She got married all of a sudden and had a baby in eight months.

PAMELA. Very suspicious.

ETHEL. But it was premature, and every time Cynthia said so, everybody said "Yes".

PAMELA. Quite right, too.

ETHEL. But it was the way they said it.

JACKY (*crossing to the easy chair* LC) Don't worry, darling— (*she removes her coat*) I shan't have a baby for at least two years —for Aunt Vera's benefit. (*She puts her coat over the back of the easy chair* LC) But we've got to get married quickly as Victor and I go to Paris in the New Year. (*She sits in the easy chair* LC) We can't help it if his father suddenly wants to open a branch there.

ETHEL. Of course you can't, darling, and it's such a good match.

PAMELA. So beneficial to the Fordyce family.

ETHEL. That's no way to speak of it. It's the uniting of two— er—families in—er—closer bonds.

PAMELA. You mean the uniting of two firms in closer bonds.

ETHEL. Pam, darling! Jacky's in *love* with Victor—aren't you, darling?

JACKY. Of course I am.

ETHEL. Of course she is.

(NICHOLAS FORDYCE *enters up* C. *He is aged about nineteen and is pleasant and amusing*)

NICHOLAS. Good afternoon, all. (*He goes to Ethel and kisses her*) Wait until you see me in my morning coat. They'll think I'm the bridegroom.

ETHEL. Have you been measured, dear?

NICHOLAS. Ran the tape over me and said I had the perfect figure. I like those chaps, so good for one's ego.

ETHEL. What a blessing one can hire those things.

NICHOLAS. Three cheers for Moss Bros! (*He moves to the table* R *and looks at the parcels*) What are these—presents?

JACKY. Yes, and it was hell getting them.

NICHOLAS (*picking up a parcel*) Any for me?

PAMELA (*rising and running to Nicholas*) Hey, not to be opened until Christmas.

(NICHOLAS *side-steps to* C. PAMELA *passes to* R *of him.*

ANNIE, *the maid, enters up* C *with a tray of tea-things. She passes between Nicholas and Pamela and bends over as she puts the tray on the coffee-table.* NICHOLAS *tosses the parcel to* PAMELA *and moves behind Annie*)

ETHEL. Thank you, Annie.

(ANNIE *straightens quickly with a yelp*)

Nick!

(NICHOLAS *shrugs and looks innocent.* ANNIE *manoeuvres herself to* L *of him and collects the coats from the easy chair* LC. PAMELA *puts the parcel on the table* R *and moves down* R)

I always say tea is such a blessing. (*She pours the tea*)

(ANNIE *exits up* C)

NICHOLAS. Yes, dear, every tea time, the same as father sniffs the coffee every morning and says "Ah! Coffee!" (*He moves to the table* R) Which of these is mine?
PAMELA. Never you mind.
NICHOLAS. I hope it's what I want.
PAMELA. It ought to be. You've dropped enough hints.
NICHOLAS. Think what a help that is. You don't have to spend weeks beforehand wondering what to buy me.
PAMELA. We never have to do that with you. You always tell us by the end of August.

(*The front door bell is heard*)

ETHEL. I wonder who that can be.
NICHOLAS. More presents. You know, Jacky, you lose on this Christmas wedding business.
PAMELS. Why?
NICHOLAS. People combine Christmas and wedding presents. I have.
PAMELA. You would.

(ANNIE *enters up* C, *leaving the door open*)

ANNIE. Excuse me, madam.
ETHEL. Yes, Annie, what is it?
ANNIE. Well, there is a woman outside who wants to see the family.
NICHOLAS. Jolly nice of her. Shoot her in.
ETHEL. What's her name?
ANNIE. A Mrs Amelia Puffin.
ETHEL. Mrs Puffin? I've never heard of her. Has anybody?

(*The others shake their heads*)

NICHOLAS. No, but let's have her in. I'd like to meet a Puffin.
ETHEL. Did she say what she wanted, Annie?
ANNIE. No, madam, just to see the family.
NICHOLAS. A very laudable wish.
PAMELA. Perhaps she is from the dressmaker's.
JACKY (*rising and moving to the fireplace*) Then she would have asked for me.
ETHEL. A friend of Victor's family, perhaps?
NICHOLAS. Meanwhile, Mrs Puffin waits without. Anxious to meet us, puffin' to meet us. Show her in, Annie.
ETHEL. Yes, show her in, Annie.

(Mrs Amelia Puffin *sidles in unannounced up* c. *She is a poor, but neatly dressed woman aged about forty-five, carrying a small shopping bag. She looks slightly mournful, but is not overawed by the assembled family. She speaks with a strong Cockney accent*)

Annie. Yes, madam. (*She turns to go and almost bumps into Mrs Puffin*)

Mrs Puffin (*glancing around*) Good afternoon. 'Ow are yer?

(Annie *moves up* LC *and stares at Mrs Puffin*)

Ethel (*taken aback*) Oh—er—how do you do? I'm Mrs Fordyce.

Mrs Puffin. Yes, I know. (*She points to the others in turn*) And that's Mr Nicholas, that's Miss Pamela and that's Miss Jacqueline.

Nicholas. Blimey!

Jacky. Won't you sit down?

Mrs Puffin. Thank you very much. (*She crosses to the easy chair* LC, *sits and puts her bag on the floor* R *of the chair*)

Ethel. Annie, fetch another cup and saucer.

(Annie *exits up* C)

Mrs Puffin. Ta ever so. I wouldn't say no to a cuppa tea. Though I didn't call 'ere for that. I couldn't get 'ere before, and as it was, I very near didn't come. Alf told me not to. He said . . .

Pamela. Who did?

Mrs Puffin. My old man. "Mark my words", 'e said, "no good will come of it, 'Melia", but I said I must go, so I did, and 'ere I am.

Ethel (*faintly*) Yes.

(Annie *enters with a cup, saucer and spoon and puts them on the tray*)

Oh—er—thank you, Annie.

(Annie *exits up* C)

Nicholas (*moving to* R *of Mrs Puffin*) But how do you know us?

Pamela (*moving down* R *of Nicholas*) I don't think we know you.

Ethel (*pouring a cup of tea for Mrs Puffin*) Really, Mrs—er . . .

Mrs Puffin. Puffin. Silly name, isn't it? Still, I took 'im and 'is name. Now there's seven little Puffins.

(Ethel *holds out the cup of tea to* Pamela, *who takes it, picks up the sugar basin and crosses to Mrs Puffin*)

Nicholas. All puffing merrily along, we hope.

Mrs Puffin. Oh, yes. (*She takes the tea from Pamela*) Ta. Two knobs, please.

(Pamela *puts two lumps of sugar in the cup, returns the basin to the tray and stands down* R *of Nicholas*)

(*She stirs her tea and holds the cup with her little finger delicately poised*)

Now, I bet you're all wonderin' why I'm 'ere.
NICHOLAS. Well, a bit.
ETHEL. I do think some explanation is necessary.
MRS PUFFIN (*handsomely*) And you shall 'ave it, only, first, is the wedding on?
ETHEL. Oh, of course it's on. I mean, of course it's going to take place. Really, Mrs Puffin . . .
MRS PUFFIN. Ah, but who to? Don't tell me, 'cos I might be too late—then again I might be too early. If I'm too early—all right. If I'm too late—all right.
NICHOLAS. In fact, it doesn't matter a damn either way.
MRS PUFFIN. Oh, but it does, dear. Oh, yes. Now, is the bridegroom . . .? Now, don't tell me—I've got to think. (*She thinks deeply, nodding her head*) Ah! I know—it's Victor Parker.
ETHEL. Yes, it is, but I . . .
MRS PUFFIN. Then I'm early.
NICHOLAS. Hooray!
ETHEL (*rising and moving down* R) Really, Mrs Puffin, I fail to see what business this is of yours. You force your way into this house, and . . .
MRS PUFFIN (*rising; indignantly*) Ooh, I never. (*She picks up her bag, puts her cup on the tray and moves to* L *of the sofa*) I got asked in and given a cup of tea.
ETHEL. Whether you were or not . . .
JACKY. Please, Mother. Mrs Puffin, you must have some very good reason for coming here. Won't you tell us why?
PAMELA (*crossing to* R *of the easy chair* LC) Yes, please.
ETHEL. Children, I fail to see . . .
NICHOLAS. Quiet, Mother! Mrs Puffin, the floor is yours.

(NICHOLAS *helps* MRS PUFFIN *to sit on the sofa, at the left end of it*)

MRS PUFFIN (*to Nicholas; chuckling*) You're a one, you are. (*She puts her bag on the floor* L *of the sofa*) Well, it's about this wedding. I don't know 'ow to say this—I'm sorry . . .
ETHEL (*bristling*) Why?
MRS PUFFIN. It won't 'appen.

(*There is a stupefield silence in the midst of which* MRS PUFFIN *picks up her cup and calmy drinks her tea*)

NICHOLAS (*sighing*) Bang goes my morning coat. Ah, well!
ETHEL (*indignantly*) Mrs—Mrs—whoever you are, how dare you come here and—and . . . Will you please leave at once.
MRS PUFFIN. Well, I like that! 'Ere I am, come all the way from Clapham . . .
NICHOLAS. Junction or Common?
MRS PUFFIN. Junction. Of course, if you don't want me to stay, I'll go, but I must say . . . (*She puts down her cup*)

ETHEL (*crossing to the door up* C) There is no need to say anything. You have said far too much already. This is no business of yours. Good-bye, Mrs Puffin.

JACKY (*with a step towards Ethel*) Please, Mother!

(PAMELA *moves to* L *of Ethel*)

Mrs Puffin must have some good reason for coming here.

NICHOLAS. Of course she has. The wedding is off.

(NICHOLAS *moves to* ETHEL, *leads her to the easy chair* LC, *sits her in it and stands* R *of her*)

ETHEL. It's not off. Don't be so ridiculous.

PAMELA. Oh, be quiet, Nick! Mrs Puffin, what does this mean?

MRS PUFFIN (*rising and moving* C) Why are you all getting so excited? There's no need.

NICHOLAS. No need at all. Let's all keep calm and collected.

ETHEL (*outraged*) Calm and collected!

MRS PUFFIN. Calm and collected. I remember them very words. There's no need to get excited, you know. It's all 'appened before. Word for word.

JACKY. What has?

NICHOLAS. I know! "I have been here before". Good old Priestley.

MRS PUFFIN. Who's 'e, when 'e's at 'ome with 'is boots off? There's no Priestley. You're not all 'ere, yet, but 'e doesn't come into this.

ETHEL (*with rising voice*) Mrs Puffin, will you please . . .

NICHOLAS. Explain something soon, otherwise my mother will have a fit.

PAMELA. So will I.

JACKY. Please, Mrs Puffin. And be quiet, all of you. After all, this does concern me.

NICHOLAS (*crossing to the fireplace*) I'm the best man, Pam's the chief bridesmaid, mother will be well to the fore, and Victor's the bridegroom . . .

MRS PUFFIN. 'E ain't.

NICHOLAS. Oh, yes, I was forgetting—'e ain't. (*He sits in the easy chair down* L)

MRS PUFFIN. No, 'e ain't. I can't for the life of me remember at the moment who is. That's a bit vague, but it'll come. It's coming clearer now. (*She sits on the sofa*)

ETHEL. Will you please tell me why you are here?

MRS PUFFIN (*settling herself comfortably*) Well, it's like this.

(PAMELA *kneels* L *of Mrs Puffin*)

I felt it my duty to come. Alf argued and said "No". I said, "Yes, Alf, it's the 'and of Fate. Mrs. Fordyce is a mother and so am I".

NICHOLAS. Seven times.
MRS PUFFIN. "You won't get thanked, 'Melia", 'e says, "like as not they'll show you the door".
ETHEL. Highly probable.
MRS PUFFIN. "Well", I said, "that's a bridge we'll cross when we come to it", as the Vicar said when 'e mislaid 'is upper set. (*She enjoys her joke enormously*) "Look at it this way", I said, "If it was Elsie instead of Miss Jacqueline, I'd be grateful".
PAMELA. Who is Elsie?
MRS PUFFIN. My eldest. Going to get spliced in the summer to George Wilkins, as nice a lad as . . .
ETHEL. Mrs Puffin, will you please come to the point?
MRS PUFFIN. Well, I am. This 'ere wedding will 'ave to be cancelled, 'cos it ain't going to take place.

(*This announcement causes* JACKY *to wander thoughtfully up* C *and then behind the sofa*)

So I came to warn you, to save you all that expense. I bet you've invited near a hundred people. You got the Church, the organ, the flowers, the cake, and a bit of a do afterwards—and all for what? Nothing!
JACKY (*moving and sitting* R *of Mrs Puffin on the sofa*) But, Mrs Puffin, you haven't told me why, yet.
MRS PUFFIN. You poor lamb, I 'aven't, 'ave I? (*Impressively*) Well, a couple of nights ago I 'ad a dream.
ETHEL. A dream? This is too much. I will not listen to such rubbish.
MRS PUFFIN. 'Alf a mo'. You ain't 'eard nothing yet. You ain't 'alf got a shock coming to you, you 'ave. Three nights ago I 'ad this dream. I saw this 'ouse, this room, the family, everyone, and what 'appened in my dream is 'appening now, word for word. You see, in my dream I was kind of two people. Me, myself, if you know what I mean, and what was 'appening, if you can understand me.
ETHEL. No.
MRS PUFFIN. You know, you're making it very difficult. I saw this 'ouse, twenty-three Henley Road, as clear as anything. So I said to Alf the next day, "I must go and see 'em and tell 'em about it". He said, "Don't do that, they won't like". So I said, "I'll go and look as the 'ouse. If the 'ouse is there that'll prove it". So up I comes and there's the 'ouse. Then while I'm outside —(*to Nicholas*) out you popped.
NICHOLAS. Did I?
MRS PUFFIN. I said at once "Mr Nicholas".
NICHOLAS. And what did I say?
MRS PUFFIN. Nothing. You didn't see me. I thought, "Ere's a funny 'ow do you do". So I waited. And what d'you think 'appened?

NICHOLAS. Someone else popped out.

MRS PUFFIN. You're right. Miss Pamela popped out and went down the road. I knew 'er at once. "Funnier and funnier", I said to myself. Just then a maid, or such like, came out from next door.

NICHOLAS. One bustling hive of activity.

MRS PUFFIN. So I said to 'er, "Excuse me, that's the Fordyce 'ouse, ain't it?" She said "Yes". So I said, "Excuse me, is Miss Jacqueline getting married soon?" And she said, "Yes, on Boxing Day". You could 'ave knocked me down with a coal 'ammer. So I went back to Alf and said, "Blimey, it's true! What'll I do now?" An' 'e said—well you know what men are —"Forget it".

ETHEL. It's a pity you didn't follow his advice. I have never heard such nonsense. You said yourself you came up here yesterday and made enquiries, consequently you knew the wedding was taking place. Really, Mrs Puffin . . .

MRS PUFFIN. 'Ow was it I knew who you all was the minute I came into the room?

ETHEL. From your enquiries. Really, Jacky, this is too much.

JACKY. Mrs. Puffin, you must admit that so far you haven't proved anything.

MRS PUFFIN. No, but, Miss Jacqueline, a lot of this dream is very 'azy. It was as clear as daylight when I dreamt it, but it's coming back clearer every minute. F'rinstance—I know what 'appens now. I remember. A telegraph boy comes with a telegram, your maid brings it in, and it's for—(*she nods to Nicholas*) 'im.

NICHOLAS. Who is it from?

MRS PUFFIN. Blimey, you don't 'alf want your money's worth. (*She thinks deeply*) I remember. It's from Stan, 'e can't come tonight. There.

(NICHOLAS *rises*)

PAMELA. That's ridiculous!

NICHOLAS. It isn't. I'm meeting Stanley Cooper tonight. He's coming up from Essex.

ETHEL. I don't believe it.

NICHOLAS. But it's true.

ETHEL. I don't mean you. I mean her.

(*The front door bell rings*)

JACKY (*rising and moving down* R) If this should be true . . .

PAMELA (*rising and moving up* R) It can't be.

MRS PUFFIN. It is, you know.

ETHEL. How could this woman possibly know that you were meeting a friend named Stanley Cooper tonight?

(ANNIE *enters up* C *with a telegram on a salver. She pauses for a moment at the top of the steps as the others turn and look at her, then she crosses to Nicholas*)

ANNIE. For you, sir.

NICHOLAS (*taking the telegram*) Thank you, Annie. (*He stands holding the telegram*)

   (*There is a silence.*
   ANNIE *exits up* C)

Y'know, it's not much use opening this; Stan can't come, that's all.

ETHEL. I don't believe it. Open it.

JACKY. Please, Nick. This is important.

NICHOLAS. Very well. (*He tears open the envelope, takes out the telegram and reads it*) "Regret cannot come tonight. Will telephone tomorrow. Stanley". Strewth!

MRS PUFFIN. There you are.

ETHEL. This woman is in league with the G.P.O.

JACKY. What else do you know, Mrs Puffin?

MRS PUFFIN. I know you won't marry this bloke—Victor Parker.

ETHEL (*rising*) You can't come here and disrupt this household. My daughter knows who she is in love with and who she'll marry.

MRS PUFFIN. Does she?

ETHEL. Of course.

MRS PUFFIN (*to Jacky*) Do you, dear?

JACKY. If I don't marry, Victor, who do I marry? There's nothing to stop the wedding.

ETHEL. And nothing will.

JACKY. I wonder.

PAMELA. Jacky, what do you mean?

JACKY. Well, all this is rather strange.

NICHOLAS. Very odd.

ETHEL. Yes, but what does Victor do that Jacky won't—I mean—that you say she won't marry him? Victor is a nice, steady, reliable young man.

MRS PUFFIN. Oh, I remember 'im. Nice young chap, but 'e ain't the romantical type.

NICHOLAS. Was your Alf?

MRS PUFFIN (*chuckling*) 'E 'ad 'is moments.

NICHOLAS. Yes, seven of them.

ETHEL. Victor is a worthy young man, and my daughter will be very happy with him, and I'll thank you, Mrs Puffin, to mind your own business and go. The idea! (*She moves up* C)

JACKY (*to Mrs Puffin*) If the wedding doesn't take place . . .

ETHEL (*stopping abruptly and turning*) Jacky!

JACKY. I said "if"—why doesn't it?

MRS PUFFIN. You're swep' off your feet.
JACKY. Swept off my feet? Who by?
MRS PUFFIN. The other bloke what's coming.
ETHEL. What bloke? I mean—who?
MRS PUFFIN. I can't remember.
ETHEL. There! What did I say?
NICHOLAS. What did you say?
ETHEL. What? What I've been saying all along. This is ridiculous.
NICHOLAS (*waving the telegram*) Is this?
MRS PUFFIN. Yes, is that? I remembered that, and give me time and I'll remember the other bloke. 'Ere, and I'll tell you something else. I came straight in 'ere, didn't I? I never been 'ere before except in my dream. Well, later on I get shoved in there—(*she points to the study door down* R) and in there there's a ruddy awful clock what don't go, and it's stopped at ten to four. There!
ETHEL. That's no way to speak of my father's presentation clock.
MRS PUFFIN. No-one ain't got the right to present a clock like that to anyone.
NICHOLAS. Mrs Puffin, my heart warms to you.
ETHEL. You looked through the windows before you came to the front door. That's how you know about the clock.
MRS PUFFIN. Ho, did I? Well, your father's name was Wentworth. That's on the clock.
NICHOLAS. You know, Mother, she couldn't have read that through the window.
MRS PUFFIN. And I'll tell you something else. (*She points to Ethel*) In a minute or two your 'usband's coming in, rubbing 'is 'ands and saying, "Well, well, well! Seasonable weather we're having. Who's this?" And 'e'll mean me. And Gordon Bennett! Are we going to have trouble with 'im.
NICHOLAS (*turning to the fire*) I bet we are.
ETHEL. We are not. There will be nothing to have trouble about. You are going. (*She moves to the doors up* C) Good-bye, Mrs Puffin, thank you for calling.

(*The front door is heard to slam*)

NICHOLAS. Too late.
ETHEL (*moving and sitting in the easy chair* LC) Not a word of this to your father.
NICHOLAS (*moving* LC) Well, who is she? He does ask; she said so.
ETHEL. She's—she's—oh, who is she? Can't anyone think?

(HENRY FORDYCE *enters up* C. *He is a typical business man, very "hail fellow well met" and a back slapper*)

HENRY (*rubbing his hands vigorously*) Well, well, well! Seasonable weather we're having. (*He moves* C) Who is this?

(*There is a silence.* MRS PUFFIN *rises*)

(*To Mrs Puffin*) I'm so sorry, I don't think I know you.
MRS PUFFIN. Not yet, but you will.
HENRY (*heartily*) I'm sure I will. (*To Ethel*) Who is this lady?
ETHEL. Oh—er—yes. Henry dear, this is—er—Mrs—er . . .
MRS PUFFIN. Puffin.
HENRY (*shaking hands with Mrs Puffin*) How do you do?
ETHEL. Mrs Puffin was just going.
HENRY. Oh, good-bye. (*He shakes hands again and crosses down* R *to Jacky*) Well, how's the bride-to-be? Still busy? (*To Mrs Puffin*) You know Jacky is soon to be married?
MRS PUFFIN. Well, that's why I came to . . .
ETHEL (*hastily*) To offer her congratulations, Henry. Now, we must not keep her, she has a long way to go. Camden Town.
MRS PUFFIN. Clapham Junction.
ETHEL. Oh, yes, Clapham Junction. Such a nice place. (*She rises*) Good-bye, Mrs Puffin—so good of you to call.
MRS PUFFIN. Yes, wasn't it? All right, I'll go. But you mark my words. I'm right.
HENRY (*moving behind the sofa*) Right about what?
ETHEL. Well, Henry—Mrs Puffin—er—meant . . .
JACKY. That the wedding wouldn't take place.
ETHEL. Jacky!
HENRY. Won't take place? (*He laughs heartily, crosses to the easy chair* LC *and sits*) Of course it will. Everything is arranged, and there have been some arrangements, haven't there, Ethel darling? But everything is going smoothly.
NICHOLAS. Then here is the spanner in the works.
HENRY. Who? What?
NICHOLAS. Mrs Puffin.
ETHEL. Really, this is ridiculous. Mrs Puffin had her little joke—and . . .
NICHOLAS. We all had a jolly good laugh.
JACKY. And now we have stopped laughing. . . .
HENRY. Why?
JACKY. Because you came in.
PAMELA. Because a telegram arrived.
JACKY. And because of grandfather's presentation clock in the study which has stopped at ten to four.
PAMELA. And because Jacky is going to be swept off her feet by another man.
HENRY. Good God, who?
PAMELA. She can't remember.
JACKY. Mrs Puffin, I think you had better come and sit down again.

(MRS PUFFIN *sits on the sofa, at the left end of it*)

HENRY. You can't be swept off your feet by someone or other a week before you marry Victor. It isn't possible.

ETHEL. That's exactly what I said, dear. Now, don't let's worry over it any more. Good-bye, Mrs Puffin.

HENRY. Who is she? A fortune teller? I thought she was a friend of yours.

ETHEL. I've never seen her before.

NICHOLAS. Mrs Puffin had a dream.

HENRY. Mrs Puffin had a what?

NICHOLAS. A dream, and a jolly good one, too.

ETHEL. It was not a good one.

JACKY (*crossing to* L *of the sofa*) It was a very vivid dream, and as I am the bride, I want to hear more about it from Mrs Puffin.

NICHOLAS. If I know Mrs Puffin, we will. A lot more.

ETHEL. And if I know father, we won't.

HENRY. If it means cancelling the wedding, you're quite right, Ethel, my dear. Give me a cup of tea, please.

(ETHEL *crosses and sits* R *of Mrs Puffin on the sofa*)

ETHEL (*lifting the teapot*) There. I knew you would be sensible about it, my dear.

MRS PUFFIN. Excuse me, but is that the best tea service, or one you only use on weekdays?

ETHEL. This is our best. (*She pours a cup of tea for Henry and hands it to Jacky*)

(JACKY *passes the cup to Henry*)

MRS PUFFIN. You want to watch out then. He's going to drop that in a minute.

NICHOLAS (*trying to take the cup from Henry*) For heaven's sake, put it down and don't have any more tea, Father.

HENRY. Why on earth not?

NICHOLAS. Because you don't know Mrs Puffin.

HENRY (*incensed*) I don't want to know Mrs Puffin. I come home after a hard day in the office, slaving in the City to help this family, and I'm entitled to my cup of tea. What's come over everyone?

JACKY (*moving to* R *of Henry*) Listen, darling, it's all very simple. Mrs Puffin has come a long way to tell me I'm not going to marry Victor.

HENRY (*putting his cup on the small table* L *of his chair*) But what has she got to do with it?

JACKY. Nothing. But she had a dream.

PAMELA (*moving between Jacky and Henry*) She dreamt about this house and us, and she knew us as soon as she came in.

JACKY. It was a very vivid dream. She knew Nicky was going to receive a telegram.

NICHOLAS (*waving the telegram*) Exhibit one, in the case of the Fordyce family versus Mrs Puffin.
PAMELA. She knew about the clock in the study.
NICHOLAS. Exhibit two, which I won't produce, as we all hate the sight of it.
JACKY. She knew you were coming in rubbing your hands and saying, "Well, well, well! Seasonable weather we're having. Who is this?"
NICHOLAS (*bowing gracefully to Henry*) Exhibit three.
HENRY. Good God! I've never heard such rubbish. (*He crosses his right leg over his left and knocks his cup off the table. It falls to the floor and smashes*)

(ETHEL *rises*)

NICHOLAS. Exhibit four. Now, talk yourself out of that.
MRS PUFFIN. I knew it was going to 'appen. I saw that real vivid. Oh, spoilt the set, ain't it?

(PAMELA *crosses, kneels and picks up the broken pieces.* NICHOLAS *assists her.* JACKY *crosses to* R *of Pamela*)

ETHEL (*wailing*) Henry, how could you!
HENRY (*wrathfully*) I did not do it on purpose.
ETHEL. You could have put it on the tray.
HENRY. How the devil can I drink a cup of tea sitting here if the tray is over there?
ETHEL (*to Mrs Puffin; nearly hysterically*) Will you please go before anything else is broken?
MRS PUFFIN (*indignantly*) I didn't do nothing. 'E broke it. I've been sittin' 'ere as quiet as anything. Not that I couldn't see that coming.
ETHEL. You don't by any chance see your departure?
MRS PUFFIN. Oh no, dear, not yet; a lot's got to 'appen yet. We ain't 'eard the last of that tea set yet.
ETHEL. No!
MRS PUFFIN. I can't remember who drops it, but there ain't 'arf one 'ell of a crash.
HENRY (*rising*) Pamela, for heaven's sake, ring for Annie to come and take it away.
ETHEL. No.
HENRY. Then you take it away, Pamela.
PAMELA (*rising*) Oh, no! Oh, no!
HENRY. Then you take it, Jacky.
JACKY. Oh, no.
HENRY. Nicholas.
NICHOLAS. Not on your life. (*He sits in the easy chair down* L)
MRS PUFFIN. I'll take it.
ETHEL. No! Don't touch it. Leave it alone.

HENRY (*shouting*) But we can't sit staring at the damn thing for ever.

NICHOLAS. I know. It's left here until the evening. Victor comes in, picks it up, drops it, and is kicked out of this house for ever. (*To Mrs Puffin*) How's that?

MRS PUFFIN. No, I don't think it's that, dear.

HENRY. Then who does take the damn thing? If we only knew that we could get somebody else.

MRS PUFFIN (*squirming with embarrassment; shyly*) I can't remember. Y'see, I remember the main part of my dream, that Miss Jacky doesn't marry this Victor; but all these bits keep coming back as we go along—if you see what I mean.

HENRY. I'm damned if I do.

MRS PUFFIN. Yes, I suppose it is a bit 'ard to understand unless you know me. Y'see, you got to know me. My hubby knows me.

HENRY. Then God help him!

MRS PUFFIN. Mind you, this ain't the first dream by a long chalk, oh, dear, no. D'you know, last night I dreamt the winner at the dogs. I saw it as clear as I'm seeing you now. Good-looking bitch, too. Knew the name, too. 'Eard them shouting it in my dream.

NICHOLAS. What happened?

MRS PUFFIN. Forgot it the minute I woke up. Alf wasn't 'arf annoyed. Created something awful. "Alf", I said, "be patient. It'll come". And it did.

HENRY. When?

MRS PUFFIN. The minute I laid eyes on Mrs Fordyce. Dog's name was Ethel, too.

HENRY (*moving up* C) This woman is a menace.

JACKY (*moving to* L *of Henry*) Daddy, do you think it would be all right if . . .

HENRY. If what?

JACKY. If we cancelled the wedding.

HENRY. Cancelled the wedding! Certainly not! What will Victor say? What will his father say? Just because some woman comes here and says she had a dream. We'd be the laughing stock of the neighbourhood.

ETHEL. Of course we would. But what about my tea service?

HENRY (*collecting two cups*) Nothing will happen to your tea service. I'll prove it to you. Now, each take a cup, saucer and plate. I'll take the tray with the teapot on and the rest. We will all take them to the kitchen. Right! (*He puts the cups down with a bang*)

ETHEL. Oh, Henry, please be careful.

HENRY (*shouting*) My dear Ethel, keep calm. Now, come on everyone. Nicholas, Jacky, Pamela.

(Mrs Puffin *leans forward to pick up a cup*)

Not you, Mrs Puffin, drop it!

Ethel (*frantically*) No! Don't drop it!

Henry. Come along, Nicholas, Jacky, Pamela—cup, saucer, plate.

(Nicholas *rises. He*, Jacky *and* Pamela *collect a cup, saucer and plate*)

If the contents of the tray are equally divided, nothing can happen.

(Jacky, Nicholas *and* Pamela *move to the door up* c. Henry *picks up the tray and follows them.* Mrs Puffin *watches with interest*)

Right! Are we ready?

Nicholas. You know, I bet we look damn fools.

Henry. Never mind about that, Nicholas. Lead the way, Jacky.

(Jacky, Nicholas *and* Pamela *exit up* c)

(*He goes up the steps, stumbles on the first one, but saves himself*) There you are; all that's needed is a little organization.

(Henry *exits up* c. Mrs Puffin *and* Ethel *listen attentively.*
Henry, Jacky, Pamela *and* Nicholas *re-enter up* c. Henry *moves down* c. Jacky *goes down* rc. Pamela *stands up* r. Nicholas *crosses to the fireplace*)

Ethel. Henry, you're wonderful. I would never have thought of that.

Nicholas. But that doesn't explain Exhibits one, two, three and four.

Henry. Coincidences. (*To* Jacky) There, my dear—Mrs Puffin has been proved wrong over one thing, and she is undoubtedly wrong on another. Now, don't worry your pretty little head any more. You and Victor will be happily married next week.

Ethel. Well, I'm very glad. Good-bye, Mrs Puffin.

Henry (*crossing to Mrs Puffin*) Exactly. Go home and dream some more dreams.

Ethel. But for heaven's sake keep us out of them.

(Mrs Puffin *picks up her bag and rises*)

Nicholas. Cheerio, Mrs Puffin. It's been fun meeting you.

Mrs Puffin (*moving up* c) Bye, bye, sir.

(Ethel *sits on the sofa*)

Pamela. I don't know about fun, but it's been an experience.

(*She moves to Mrs Puffin and shakes hands with her*) Good-bye, Mrs Puffin.

JACKY. Good-bye. Thank you for coming. You meant well, I'm sure.

MRS PUFFIN. Yes, I did. But I think it's very funny. I hope you'll be very 'appy, miss. (*She shakes hands with Jacky*)

JACKY. Thank you. I hope so, too.

MRS PUFFIN. Well, I'm off.

(*There is a terrific crash of crockery off, and a scream from* ANNIE. ETHEL *screams and rises.*

ANNIE *runs in up* C)

MRS PUFFIN			There! The 'and of Fate!
ETHEL	(*together*)		My best tea service!
ANNIE			Oh, madam!
HENRY			Oh, no!

(JACKY *runs to the doors up* C)

ANNIE (*running to Ethel*) Oh, ma'am, I'm ever so sorry. I fell over Twinkle.

HENRY. That damned cat! I knew it was unlucky.

NICHOLAS. But it's a black one.

ETHEL (*to Annie*) Why didn't you leave the things on the table?

ANNIE. But I had to wash up, ma'am—I piled them on a tray and was taking them to the sink—and I fell over Twinkle.

ETHEL (*leading Annie up* C) Oh dear, oh dear, oh dear! (*She stops and turns at the top of the steps*)

(ANNIE *exits up* C)

(*To Mrs Puffin. Hysterically*) This is all your fault!

(ETHEL *exits up* C)

MRS PUFFIN. Poor soul! The 'and of Fate. (*She moves slowly to the left end of the sofa and sits*) I knew it was going to 'appen. (*She puts her bag on the floor* L *of the sofa*)

NICHOLAS (*crossing towards the telephone up* R) I'm going to ring up the tailors and cancel my morning coat.

HENRY (*intercepting Nicholas*) You're not!

NICHOLAS. I am. From now onwards I am a Puffin fan. I will take no step in the future without consulting the oracle. She may have dreamt about me. (*He kneels at Mrs Puffin's feet*) Mrs Puffin, dream about me.

MRS PUFFIN. Oh, I can't do it to order. It just 'appens.

HENRY. Why did it have to happen to us? (*He moves to* L *of Nicholas and pushes him aside*) Oh, get out of the way, Nicholas.

(NICHOLAS *rises*)

Now, Mrs Puffin, since you have been so clever, perhaps you'll explain this.

MRS PUFFIN. I'll do anything I can. I only want to 'elp.

HENRY. I must say you have been a great help.

(NICHOLAS *moves behind the sofa*)

(*To Pamela*) Now then, what was it you said, Pamela, about Jacky being swept off her feet by another man?

PAMELA (*moving above the left end of the sofa*) That's what Mrs Puffin said. "You're swept off your feet by another bloke", that's what she said.

MRS PUFFIN. My very words.

HENRY. Well, who is he?

JACKY. She can't remember. (*She moves and sits on the right arm of the easy chair* LC) This is a fine state of affairs, I must say. I'm to be swept off my feet by someone I don't know a week before my wedding to someone else. I'm not used to being swept off my feet.

HENRY. Victor did.

JACKY. I'm very fond of Victor, but . . .

NICHOLAS. But he just doesn't sweep.

HENRY. This isn't getting us anywhere. Now, Mrs Puffin, who is this other man?

MRS PUFFIN. Do you know, it's a funny thing, but I can't remember. That bit's a bit vague. It's funny 'ow bits keep on coming back all of a sudden.

HENRY. It's damned annoying! Think, Mrs Puffin, think.

MRS PUFFIN. Lummy! I am thinking. I ain't stopped thinking. I'm getting dizzy with thinking.

PAMELA. Is he tall—dark—fair?

JACKY. Short—fat?

MRS PUFFIN. No, 'e ain't short and fat.

NICHOLAS. Well, he might be. A lot of these short fat chaps are regular Don Juans.

JACKY. Oh, don't say that, Nick.

MRS PUFFIN. I can't see 'im. 'E's 'azy.

HENRY. Concentrate! Concentrate! (*He kneels in front of Mrs Puffin*)

(MRS PUFFIN *screws up her face in an agony of concentration*)

MRS PUFFIN. Oh, give over breathing on my knee caps. I do know one thing. He's connected with water.

NICHOLAS. He's a sailor! Now, do they sweep? One in every port.

PAMELA. He's something to do with water.

NICHOLAS. I know. A commercial traveller in Soda Syphons.

HENRY (*rising*) We don't know anyone remotely connected with water.

JACKY. Mrs Puffin, I'm sorry, but . . .
MRS PUFFIN (*earnestly*) Listen, miss, I know I'm right about water.
JACKY. No, it's impossible!
HENRY. Of course it's impossible. The whole damn thing is impossible.

(*The front door bell rings. There is a ghastly pause*)

NICHOLAS (*into Mrs Puffin's ear*) Exhibit five coming up?

(ANNIE *enters up* C)

ANNIE. Excuse me, sir.
HENRY. Now what is it?
PAMELA. Is it a man?
ANNIE. No, miss, it's the dressmaker.
PAMELA. Heavens! I forgot, Jacky, we've got a fitting.

(PAMELA *runs out up* C)

HENRY. Yes, of course. Now, Jacky, be sensible, forget this nonsense. Go up and have your fitting. Mrs Puffin can't remember a thing about this so-called other man. Forget all about it.
JACKY. Mrs Puffin, if you do remember will you tell me about it?
MRS PUFFIN. Don't worry. I'm on the qwee wee.
HENRY. There isn't one. (*He hustles Jacky to the door*)

(JACKY *exits up* C)

ANNIE. Mrs Fordyce is lying down with a headache, sir, and she says she isn't coming down until Mrs Puffin has left.

(ANNIE *exits up* C)

NICHOLAS (*to Mrs Puffin*) You see, you haven't exactly made a hit with my mother.
MRS PUFFIN. Well, I've done my best, I'm sure.
HENRY. Now, Mrs Puffin . . .
MRS PUFFIN. It's all right, sir. I'm still thinking.
HENRY. Well, don't; stop thinking.
MRS PUFFIN. But 'ow am I to remember if I don't think?
HENRY (*crossing down* L) Because I don't want you to think.
MRS PUFFIN. Now, look 'ere, make up your mind. One minute you're all on at me to think, now you don't want me to. Lummy, I don't know where I am.

(HENRY *crosses to Mrs Puffin, takes a deep breath and speaks in a most coaxing voice*)

HENRY. Mrs Puffin, I've been very hasty. You know how it is. I've spent a hard day in the City, working very hard. I come home, irritated and on edge, and what happens?

Mrs Puffin. There, you do want me to start thinking again?
Henry (*hastily*) No, Mrs Puffin, no. Mrs Puffin, I was rude to you.
Mrs Puffin. You were a bit snooty, weren't you?
Henry. But, Mrs Puffin, madam, you must admit I had a shock when I came in.
Mrs Puffin. And saw me.
Henry. Yes. No, no! I mean, things happened.
Nicholas. That's putting it mildly.
Henry. I wasn't prepared. I was amazed. Bewildered. I was—er . . .
Nicholas. Thunderstruck!
Henry. Thank you, Nicholas.
Nicholas. Don't mention it.
Henry. I was thunderstruck. And what happened?
Nicholas. You broke a cup and saucer, and Annie, not to be outdone, smashed the whole service.
Mrs Puffin. You know, the moment it 'appened, I knew.
Nicholas. Yes, so did we.
Henry. You see, things piled up on me, and consequently I forgot you were a guest in my house. Now, Mrs Puffin, what did I think when I came in?
Mrs Puffin. Gawd knows!
Henry (*impressively*) Madam, when I came through that door a thought went through my mind the moment I saw you. (*He crosses down* R) I said to myself, "There", I said, "there is a woman of the world".
Mrs Puffin (*coyly*) Go on! You never!
Henry (*sitting* R *of Mrs Puffin on the sofa*) Madam, I asure you it's the truth. "A woman of the world", I said, "and a mother". You are a mother?
Mrs Puffin. That's right.
Nicholas. Seven times.
Henry. Seven! Madam, allow me to congratulate you.
Mrs Puffin. Thank you very much. You're a bit late, but thanks all the same.
Henry. A pleasure. A woman of the world, Nicholas, a woman of experience.
Nicholas. Indubitably.
Mrs Puffin. Well, you can't 'ave seven kids without a bit of know how, can you?
Henry. Of course you can't, and that's why I am sure you will appreciate my position.
Mrs Puffin. Why, dear, what's your trouble?
Henry. Mrs Puffin, how old is your eldest child?
Mrs Puffin. Who? My Elsie? Getting on for twenty, and as nice a girl as you could ever wish to meet. Select and lady-like.

We brought 'er up right. As I always say, she takes after me and my side of the family. Now, my old man, salt of the earth—

HENRY. The fact that he married you proves it.

MRS PUFFIN. —but rough and ready.

HENRY. With a heart of gold.

MRS PUFFIN. You never spoke a truer word.

HENRY. I'm sure I never. But your Elsie, select and lady-like, a credit to you both.

MRS PUFFIN. Class! Oh, she's got class.

HENRY. You don't have to tell me that. That girl will do well for herself. Is she married?

MRS PUFFIN. Walking out.

HENRY. Ah, courting!

MRS PUFFIN. Not 'arf! We can't get in the front room of a night. Sitting on the sofa with the lights out. But I've no need to tell you—'ave I?

HENRY (*laughing heartily*) We are both men and women of the world.

MRS PUFFIN (*laughing*) I bet you've been over a good bit of grass in your time.

NICHOLAS. I bet he has.

HENRY. Hm! Well—between you and me, Mrs Puffin . . . (*He digs her playfully in the ribs*)

MRS PUFFIN (*reacting strongly*) I bet you were a caution!

NICHOLAS. I bet he was.

HENRY. So Elsie is courting. What's her fiancé like?

MRS PUFFIN. George Wilkins? A nice lad, ever so nice. He's a plumber. What he don't know about pipes ain't worth knowing.

HENRY. Remember that, Nicholas. If ever we need a plumber —George Wilkins.

NICHOLAS. I'll make a note of it.

MRS PUFFIN. The way he fixed our "'ow-do-you-do" was a fair treat. 'E 'adn't been going out with our Elsie for more than a month when 'e completely fixed it up. None of that. (*She makes a gesture of pulling a chain*) A little 'andle on the side. Now, if ever you fancy a little 'andle . . .

HENRY. I'll bear it in mind. When are George and Elsie getting married?

MRS PUFFIN. In the summer, sir.

HENRY. A proud day for you, Mrs Puffin. I can see you standing in the church—

MRS PUFFIN. Chapel.

HENRY. —with the organ pealing—

MRS PUFFIN. Miss Pirbright on the 'armonium.

HENRY. —listening to *Here Comes the Bride*. Suddenly, down the aisle comes Elsie, leaning on your husband's arm.

MRS PUFFIN. If I know anything about dad, 'e'll be leaning on 'er.

HENRY. There is George awaiting her, all pipes forgotten for the day. Soon they are husband and wife. You go into the vestry and sign the register, then to the strains of *The Wedding March*, George and Elsie pass down the aisle. George and Elsie united until death do them part.
MRS PUFFIN (*visibly affected*) Just like me and Mr Puffin.
HENRY. Mrs Puffin—I envy you.
MRS PUFFIN. Why? You've got a daughter, too.
HENRY. I have. Little Jacky. Mrs Puffin, Jacky is engaged to Victor Parker.
MRS PUFFIN. I know.
HENRY. Exactly. A fine upstanding young man. What George is to plumbing—Victor is to Commerce. What Elsie means to George—Jacky means to Victor. Mrs Puffin, are you going to allow this happy couple to be estranged?
MRS PUFFIN. Well, now, as I said to my Alf . . .
HENRY. Since I dandled my Jacky on my knee, I've dreamt of this day. To walk proudly up the aisle with her on my arm, saying to all the world, "This lovely child—is mine".
NICHOLAS. Seeing the lovely best man, and saying, "He, too—is mine".
MRS PUFFIN. What about this other bloke what's coming?
HENRY. Mrs Puffin, Mrs Puffin, what other bloke—er—man? Vaguely you remember him. What is he? A dream.
MRS PUFFIN. Well, my dream ain't done so bad up to now.
HENRY. Have you ever heard that dreams mean the opposite? They are sent as warnings.
MRS PUFFIN. It's a pity you didn't 'eed my warning, then your tea service wouldn't have gone for a burton.
HENRY. Ah, if only we had done! I'm afraid that was my fault. But, Mrs Puffin—now we know. If any man comes, we are prepared. (*He ostentatiously takes out his wallet and fingers a bank note*)
MRS PUFFIN (*eyeing the wallet*) I remember *that*.
HENRY. But that is all you remember.
MRS PUFFIN (*firmly*) Oh, no, it ain't. This is coming back. You offer me a fiver.
HENRY. I thought of three, as a slight compensation for your trouble.
MRS PUFFIN. But you make it five, and—half a sec—it's all coming back.
HENRY (*hastily whipping out five pounds*) Don't let any more come back, Mrs Puffin. (*He hands her the notes*)
MRS PUFFIN. I get ten eventually.
HENRY (*taking back the notes*) This is blackmail!
MRS PUFFIN. 'Cos the phone rings and it's Victor's father. He wants to 'ave a talk with you.

(*The telephone rings*)

There you are.
NICHOLAS. Mrs Puffin never fails.
HENRY. It can't be.
NICHOLAS. You should know Mrs Puffin by now.
HENRY. I know too much about Mrs Puffin.
NICHOLAS. Shall I answer it?
HENRY. Yes, do. It's probably a wrong number. (*He moves away from Mrs Puffin along the sofa seat*)

(NICHOLAS *goes to the telephone and lifts the receiver*)

MRS PUFFIN. Why 'ave you gone off me, dear?
NICHOLAS (*into the telephone*) Hullo. Hampstead five-nine-six-three . . . Who . . . Oh, yes. Just a moment. (*To Henry*) Mr Stephen Parker wishes to speak to you. (*He brings the telephone behind the sofa to Henry*)
MRS PUFFIN. I said it was 'im. Funny 'ow it keeps on coming back.

(HENRY *takes the receiver.* NICHOLAS *puts the base on the table* R)

Now if you 'ad asked me ten minutes ago what 'appened next, I'd 'ave been flummoxed.
HENRY (*into the telephone*) Hullo, Stephen, how are you? . . . Oh, fine, thanks . . . Yes, Jacky's very well, she's just having a fitting . . . You're right. It won't be long now . . .
NICHOLAS (*crossing to* C) We hope!
HENRY (*into the telephone*) Tonight? . . . Victor as well? . . .
MRS PUFFIN. Oh, I knew 'e was coming.

(HENRY *signals with a wave of his hand that* MRS PUFFIN *should be quiet. She misunderstands and waves cheerfully back*)

HENRY (*into the telephone*) We'll be delighted . . . After dinner . . . Very well . . . The papers? . . . Oh, yes. I'll have to study those, but I am sure they are all right. About eight-thirty, then. Goodbye, old man . . . 'Bye. (*He rises, moves* R *and replaces the receiver*)
NICHOLAS. You've got to hand it to her, Father. She's bang on every time.
MRS PUFFIN. Oh, I know 'e's coming round about you and 'im going into partnership.
HENRY (*moving down* R) Partnership! What do you know about the Parkers?
MRS PUFFIN. I know 'em both.
HENRY. Know them both?
MRS PUFFIN. 'Course I do. Saw 'em in my dream. Tell you what they look like. (*She gives descriptions of the actors playing the parts*)
NICHOLAS. Blooming uncanny, isn't it? (*He goes to the table* R, *picks up the telephone and replaces it on the table up* R)
HENRY. It's nothing of the sort. Now, look here, Mrs Puffin,

see how much you can forget for ten pounds. (*He hastily counts out ten pounds*)

Mrs Puffin. Thank you very much, sir. At the moment I know I take it.

Henry. Of course you take it. Here. (*He thrusts the notes into her hand*)

Mrs Puffin. But what 'appens afterwards?

Henry. Nothing. You go home.

   (Annie *enters up* c)

(*He crosses to Annie*) Well, what is it?

Annie (*sotto voce*) It's Mrs Fordyce, sir.

Henry (*sotto voce*) Well, what about her?

Annie (*sotto voce*) She wants to know if . . . (*She hesitates*)

Henry (*loudly*) Well, speak up—if what?

Annie. If Mrs Puffin has left yet, and if not, when?

Mrs Puffin (*rising*) I can take an 'int. (*She picks up her bag*)

Henry. She's just leaving, Annie. Go and tell Mrs Fordyce that.

Annie. Yes, sir.

   (Annie *exits up* c)

Henry. Now, Mrs Puffin, good-bye. You've forgotten everything.

Mrs Puffin. Good-bye, sir. Thank you very much.

Henry. Show Mrs Puffin out, Nicholas. (*He crosses to the fireplace*)

Mrs Puffin. Good-bye, Mr Nicholas. (*She shakes hands with Nicholas, goes towards the doors up* c, *then stops dead and looks at the picture hanging over the mantelpiece*) Ooh, I say! That's queer. Something's gone wrong somewhere.

Henry. You don't say! What now?

Mrs Puffin (*indicating the picture*) Well, you see that picture. In my dream when Victor and his father arrive 'ere, that picture ain't there.

Henry (*very cheerfully*) Well, there we are, Mrs Puffin, that proves you can be wrong. That picture has always been there and always will be. Goodnight, Mrs Puffin.

   (Mrs Puffin *turns to go. The picture falls*)

Mrs Puffin (*glancing back*) Ah, that's better.

        Quick Curtain

ACT II

Scene—*The same. Later that evening.*
When the Curtain *rises, it is just after eight o'clock. The window curtains are closed, the light in the hall is on, but the room is lit only by the flickering light of the fire.* Ethel *and* Pamela *enter up* c.

Ethel (*switching on the wall brackets by the switch* r *of the door*) If your father mentions that Puffin woman again, I'll scream. (*She moves down* c)

(Jacky *enters up* c)

Pamela (*moving up* r) He just wanted to make sure that no-one would let Victor or his father know of her visit. (*She switches on the table-lamp up* r)

Ethel. But surely once is enough.

Jacky (*crossing to the fireplace*) You know father. (*She takes a cigarette from the box on the mantelpiece, and lights it*)

Ethel. We had Puffin for soup, Puffin for chicken . . .

Pamela. Puffin for sweet, and Nicholas is no doubt getting Puffin with his brandy.

Jacky. And in between, Annie got Puffin as well. (*She switches on the table-lamp up* l)

Ethel. If he tells Annie never to admit that woman again, she'll give in her notice.

(Annie *enters up* c, *carrying a tray of coffee*)

Jacky (*her voice indicating that Annie is there*) Well, let's forget her over coffee. (*She sits in the easy chair* lc)

Ethel. Thank you, Annie. (*She sits on the sofa*)

(Annie *puts the tray on the coffee-table in silence*)

Pamela. Of course, the only one father is afraid of is Nick.

(Annie *exits up* c)

Ethel (*pouring coffee*) I'm sure Nicholas will behave himself.

Pamela. Father isn't, and we all know Nick; he is bound to put his foot in it.

Ethel (*handing Pamela a cup of coffee over the back of the sofa*) I'm sure he'll do whatever your father says.

Pamela (*crossing to Jacky*) He'll start with the best intentions in the world. (*She hands the coffee to Jacky*) You know, it's a pity he's not meeting Stanley Cooper this evening. (*She moves to* l *of the sofa*)

Jacky. Funny how she knew about that telegram and about everything else.

ETHEL. If you're referring to my tea service—don't. (*She hands a cup of coffee to Pamela*)
JACKY. But it was funny.
ETHEL. There is nothing funny about a very good tea service being smashed to smithereens.
JACKY. But she didn't smash it.
ETHEL. She was instrumental. (*She pours coffee for herself*)
JACKY. She only knew it was going to happen, like the other things.
ETHEL. No other things are going to happen. That woman admitted to your father, after a long interrogation, that she was wrong.
JACKY. But she wasn't.
PAMELA. Neither was she wrong about the telegram.
JACKY. Or about the clock in the study.
ETHEL. Every study has a clock, and every house has at least one clock that doesn't go. I don't know why, but they do.
JACKY. But ours *was* in the study.
PAMELA. And it *had* stopped at ten to four.
ETHEL. Jacky, I don't want to discuss Mrs Puffin or her dream again. No-one knows how much I suffered this afternoon.
PAMELA. I rather enjoyed it on the whole. One wondered what she was going to say next.
ETHEL. She said quite enough. Quite enough! (*She picks up her coffee, rises and moves down* R) Now, I must check through the invitations and find out who has accepted and who hasn't. Tell your father where I am when he comes in.

(ETHEL *exits down* R)

PAMELA (*crossing and putting her cup on the table* R) Oh, what a day it's been.

(JACKY *sits holding her cup, deep in thought*)

I said—what a day it's been.

(JACKY *is silent*)

Jacky! (*She crosses to Jacky and kneels* R *of her*) Come back to earth.
JACKY. Oh, sorry, Pam. What did you say?
PAMELA. I said what a day it has been.
JACKY. Yes.
PAMELA. Are you thinking—about Mrs Puffin?
JACKY. One can hardly forget her. Apart from what happened this afternoon, father has spent the entire evening reminding us to forget. Completely spoilt my dinner.
PAMELA. That's typical of daddy. He spoilt his own, as well. Jacky, did you really believe her?
JACKY. No, of course not. Did you?

PAMELA (*loyally*) No, of course not, and there couldn't be anyone but Victor, could there?
JACKY. Not connected with water, a week before the wedding.
PAMELA. But in any case there couldn't be.
JACKY. No, of course not.
PAMELA (*enthusiastically*) Of course, he's not exactly good-looking but he's got wonderful qualities. He's so fine and so dependable.
JACKY (*smiling*) He'll be a most popular brother-in-law.
PAMELA. Oh, yes.

(NICHOLAS *enters up* C)

NICHOLAS. I have escaped from father.
JACKY. What do you mean—escaped?
NICHOLAS (*moving and sitting on the sofa*) You heard him at dinner to everyone. (*He pours himself a cup of coffee*) Well—I had him—alone ever since.
PAMELA. Puffin?
NICHOLAS. Like hell!
PAMELA (*to Jacky*) I told you so.
NICHOLAS. He's getting me so nervous I'm getting a complex. The more I'm told not to say a thing, the more I want to. I'm funny that way.
PAMELA (*rising*) You are funny anyway. (*She crosses to* R *and picks up her coffee*) But don't worry, only one person will give the show away.
NICHOLAS. Oh, Gawd, no!
PAMELA. Yes—daddy. He will be so anxious to keep us quiet that he will forget and talk about her himself.
NICHOLAS. I can see we are in for a very jolly evening, trying to stifle father while he tries to stifle us.
JACKY. Why should he be stifled?
NICHOLAS } (*together*) { (*Startled*) Eh?
PAMELA } { What?
JACKY. After all, it really concerns Victor and me; why shouldn't he know?
NICHOLAS. But you don't tell a chap you are going to be swept off your feet by another chap a week before your wedding to the first chap. He might be superstitious. Is he?
JACKY. I don't know.
NICHOLAS. I shouldn't tell him. He might be upset. I couldn't imagine Victor having a jolly good laugh over it. You could tell him on your honeymoon, but choose your moment, of course; I mean, time and place for everything.
JACKY. Perhaps you are right.
NICHOLAS. Anyway, Mrs Puffin's gone. (*He looks around*) I hope.

(HENRY *enters up* C)

HENRY (*moving down* C) Ah, coffee! Where's your mother?
JACKY (*rising and crossing to the sofa*) In the study, checking the invitations. (*She puts her cup on the tray, sits on the sofa and pours coffee for Henry*)
HENRY. That's right. Everything carries on as normal, just as if that woman never came.
NICHOLAS (*rising and crossing to the fireplace*) Here we go again.
HENRY. We are not going again. But I don't want this family to be disrupted by that woman's visit. The poor creature was probably . . . (*He taps his head*) Anyhow, she at last admitted her mistake and left.
NICHOLAS. She admitted it—er—handsomely—so let's forget her, and on with the nuptials.
JACKY (*rising and taking the cup of coffee to Henry*) What's Victor's father coming here for?
HENRY (*taking the coffee*) On business. I have to glance through the final deeds of partnership.

(*The front door bell rings.* JACKY *and* PAMELA *react*)

Ah, that's probably them now. (*He moves up* C) A little early, but all the better. (*He moves down* C) Now, remember, not a word.
NICHOLAS. Our lips are sealed.
HENRY. Good! Stephen and I will go into the study, you, too, Nicholas, as Junior Partner. (*To Pamela*) No doubt you and your mother can find something to do elsewhere. (*Jovially*) I expect Jacky and Victor have plenty to talk about; I mean their future. And a very bright future it's going to be. Annie's a long time opening that door. (*He moves behind the easy chair* LC) See what's happened, Nicholas.

(JACKY *and* PAMELA *move up* R. NICHOLAS *crosses to the doors up* C *and looks into the hall*)

NICHOLAS. Nobody there.
HENRY (*moving to the fireplace*) That's funny. I could have sworn I heard the bell.
NICHOLAS (*calling*) Annie. Annie.

(ANNIE *enters up* C)

Annie, who was that at the front door a moment ago?
ANNIE. Her!
HENRY (*moving up* LC) Who?
ANNIE. Her, sir.
HENRY. You don't mean . . . ?
ANNIE. Yes, sir, I do.
PAMELA. Mrs Puffin? Where is she?
ANNIE. Gone, miss.
JACKY. What did she want?
ANNIE. To see the family, miss.

NICHOLAS. And what did you say?
ANNIE. No. I said it was more than my job was worth.
HENRY. Quite right, too. Then what did she say?
ANNIE. "What is to be, will be. You can't escape fate", sir.
HENRY. I'm very pleased with you, Annie. Don't let her in if she comes back. Good heavens, she mustn't meet the Parkers. (*He crosses to the fireplace*)
NICHOLAS (*solemnly*) "What is to be, will be. You can't escape fate."
HENRY. This is no time for levity.

(*The front door bell rings*)

NICHOLAS. Now, who is that? Puffin or the Parkers?
HENRY. Go and see, Annie.

(ANNIE *exits up* C. *The others wait expectantly*)

NICHOLAS (*after a moment's silence*) "There's a breathless 'ush in the Close tonight . . ."

(ANNIE *enters up* C)

ANNIE. It's her again, sir.
HENRY (*moving above the easy chair* LC) Get rid of her, Annie, get rid of her.
ANNIE. I've closed the door, sir. I can't do more.
HENRY. Oh, she's gone?
ANNIE. No, she isn't. She's parked herself on the doorstep, and she says she's going to stay there, and if you want to get rid of her you'll have to shift her yourself. I'm going back to the kitchen.
HENRY. Take a week's notice.
ANNIE. Too late! I've just given it.

(ANNIE *exits up* C)

NICHOLAS. What a carry on!
HENRY. The Parkers will be here in ten minutes. Nicholas, go out to her.
NICHOLAS (*crossing down* R) Oh, no! Not me. You go.
JACKY (*moving to the door up* C) I'll go.
HENRY. No, Jacky, I forbid it.
JACKY (*as she exits*) Too late. I've gone.

(JACKY *exits up* C)

PAMELA. Now what will happen? (*She moves to Nicholas*) Oh Nick, you should have gone.
NICHOLAS. I like that! It's nothing to do with me. Anyway I'm pro-Puffin.
HENRY. You are nothing of the sort. (*He moves to the fireplace*

Well, unless Jacky wants her marriage to be ruined, she will get rid of her before the Parkers arrive.

(JACKY *and* MRS PUFFIN *enter up* C)

MRS PUFFIN (*moving* C) Hallo, I'm back again.

HENRY (*moving down* LC; *exploding*) Mrs Puffin, I told you not to come back. Jacky, I forbade her to enter this house again. Mrs Puffin, you have got to go.

MRS PUFFIN. I can't.

JACKY (*moving above the easy chair* LC) We can't leave her on the doorstep, Father.

NICHOLAS. "What is to be, will be. You can't escape fate."

MRS PUFFIN. You never spoke a truer word.

JACKY. There you are, you see.

HENRY. I don't give a damn about Fate. Will you please go. I'll—I'll—call the police.

MRS PUFFIN. Oh, no, you don't do that. A lot of things 'appen—

HENRY. Oh, no!

MRS PUFFIN. —but you don't call the police.

PAMELA (*moving to the left end of the sofa*) But what happens, Mrs Puffin?

MRS PUFFIN. Oh, a lot, miss. I meet the Parkers.

HENRY. For the last time, you do *not*!

MRS PUFFIN. But I do.

NICHOLAS. You see! "What is to be will be. You can't . . ."

HENRY. If you make that damn silly remark again, I shall do something desperate.

(NICHOLAS *sits on the right arm of the sofa*)

MRS PUFFIN. Now, why don't you be calm, Mr Fordyce, and let's talk the matter over.

HENRY (*crossing down* L) We will do no such thing.

JACKY (*moving to* R *of Henry; raising her voice*) But we must. You seem to overlook the fact that this matter concerns me and my future, and I have a right to know. And I will.

HENRY (*deflated*) Eh? But, look here—Jacky—but, can't you see—oh, my God! Say something, Nicholas.

NICHOLAS (*simply*) Rhubarb.

JACKY (*moving to* L *of Mrs Puffin*) Now, Mrs Puffin, why did you come back?

MRS PUFFIN. Well, you see, ducks—I 'ad to come back. In a manner of speaking, I was drawn 'ere, as you might say.

HENRY. Not by me you weren't.

MRS PUFFIN (*ignoring Henry*) After 'e 'ad given me the money, I thought . . .

JACKY. After what?

Mrs Puffin. After your dad gave me ten quid to keep my mouth shut.

Jacky (*with a step towards Henry*) Father!

Pamela. Oh, Daddy! You said at dinner Mrs Puffin had left because she was mistaken.

Henry. All I said—what I mean—if you must know . . . Oh, why did this bloody woman have to dream about us!

Mrs Puffin (*incensed*) That's no way to speak about a lady. I'm giving myself a lot of trouble coming 'ere, and old Alf will be creating something shocking 'cos I ain't got 'is tea. I ain't been 'ome yet.

Henry. But there's nothing to stop you.

Mrs Puffin. Don't you worry about me. Your Missis will be popping out of there soon— (*she points to the door down* R) and you'll 'ave to cope with 'er.

(Henry *sinks into the easy chair down* L, *with his head in his hands*)

Nicholas (*helpfully*) And you see, Dad, she never knew mother was in there. Nobody told her, and if she says mother's going to pop out soon—pop out she will.

Jacky (*moving to Mrs Puffin*) Carry on, Mrs Puffin. My father bribes you with ten pounds.

Mrs Puffin. I'm ever so sorry about that, miss. But it 'appened in my dream. I mean—I couldn't escape it, I 'ad to take the money, then I left. Well, I started walking back to the Underground when—click . . . (*She snaps her fingers*)

Nicholas. Click?

Mrs Puffin. Click! I can't do it with my gloves on, but click. A bit more came clear. Y'know, I'd be ever so much 'appier if it all came back at once, but it don't.

Nicholas. Very aggravating.

Mrs Puffin. Oh, it is. Y'see, out there— (*she waves her hand vaguely into the distance*) I can see no wedding to this Victor, I see your sister swep' off her feet, but I can't remember 'is name or what 'e looks like. But at the moment, I'm up to date, so to speak.

Jacky. And what does that mean?

Mrs Puffin. I've brought the money back. (*She dives into her bag, produces the money and hands it to Jacky*) I saw myself 'anding it back, after 'aving the door shut in my face. I knew you'd open the door next, and I'd come in. You see, it's all 'appening. Your ma is coming out in a minute, the Parkers arrive, and I get pushed in the study.

Henry (*eagerly*) And after that?

Mrs Puffin. I'm blowed if I remember.

Henry. Then you don't meet the Parkers.

Mrs Puffin. But I must do; I know what they look like.

NICHOLAS. It doesn't seem much use popping her into the study if she's going to pop out again.

MRS PUFFIN. But it must 'appen. Otherwise, where are we?

NICHOLAS. I don't know, and I'm damn sure my father can't tell you.

MRS PUFFIN (*to Jacky*) You see, miss, it's me conscience, I can't bear to think of me 'aving been warned, so to speak, and not passing it on to you.

JACKY. That's all right, Mrs Puffin. I deeply appreciate all you have done for us.

HENRY (*rising; spluttering*) You deeply appreciate—your life—ruined—we're all ruined—there'll be a scandal—because of this—this—complete stranger—comes into our lives with some cock-and-bull story. (*He moves down* L)

MRS PUFFIN (*crossing to Henry*) Cock-and-bull story! Oh, is it? In a moment your Missis comes out of there saying, "Henry, did we send an invitation to the Tomlinsons"? Then she sees me, and then a lot more trouble starts. But I'm prepared, I know what's going to 'appen, but you don't.

PAMELA. Mrs Puffin, don't you think you ought to go and hide—or something?

MRS PUFFIN. I can't, love, you see that never 'appened.

(ETHEL *enters down* R, *carrying a sheaf of papers*)

ETHEL (*crossing to* C) Henry, did we send an invitation to the Tomlinsons? (*She glances at Mrs Puffin*) Oh, good evening. (*She passes on, stops, turns and shrieks*) Henry! It's that woman again.

MRS PUFFIN. Good evening.

HENRY. Now, keep calm.

ETHEL. I thought you had gone for good.

MRS PUFFIN. I 'ad, but I came back.

ETHEL. Henry, will you get rid of her before I have hysterics?

NICHOLAS (*rising and moving to* R *of Ethel*) Hysterics? (*To Mrs Puffin*) does she?

MRS PUFFIN. At the moment, she's only kind of trying it on. Later on I'm not quite sure. Any'ow, I'll give you plenty of warning.

NICHOLAS (*leading Ethel to the sofa*) There, Mother, you won't get hysterical yet—

(ETHEL *sits on the sofa*)

—and if you're going to, we'll give you plenty of warning. (*He sits* R *of Ethel on the sofa*)

ETHEL. Even my own children turn against me.

PAMELA (*moving to* L *of Ethel*) Mother, everything will be all right.

ETHEL. How can it be with her in the house? How did she get in in the first place?

HENRY (*moving to Jacky*) Jacky brought her in, strictly against my orders.
ETHEL. Jacky! You of all people to upset me.
HENRY (*to Jacky*) There, you have upset your mother. I hope you're thoroughly ashamed of yourself.
JACKY. Considering you tried to bribe Mrs Puffin before dinner, I hope you're thoroughly ashamed of yourself. (*Realizing she has given Henry away, she moves away up* R)
ETHEL. Bribed? Bribed? Did you give her money, Henry?
HENRY. All I did was . . . If you will understand one thing . . . Before dinner I thought . . .
ETHEL. Did you give her money, Henry?
HENRY. Yes.
ETHEL. Henry, how could you? How much?
HENRY. Oh, a pound or two.
MRS PUFFIN. Ten pounds.
ETHEL. Henry!
MRS PUFFIN. But I brought it back. You see it was my conscience, and . . .
ETHEL (*rising and moving to* R *of Mrs Puffin*) I am not interested in your conscience. Henry, you said she left because she was mistaken. Ten pounds! Now, you've brought it back, go. (*She crosses down* R) Nobody wants you here.
HENRY. But they do. Jacky wants her here. Jacky invited her in.
ETHEL. Jacky, tell her to go. Henry, Pam, Nick—I think I'm going to faint.
NICHOLAS (*to Mrs Puffin*) Faint, Mrs Puffin?
MRS PUFFIN. No faint.
NICHOLAS (*rising and moving to Ethel*) No faint, Mother. Mrs Puffin will warn us.
MRS PUFFIN. That I will. In fact, I will now. The Parkers arrive in a minute.
HENRY. The Parkers! (*He crosses to Jacky*) Jacky, will you please do something.
JACKY. I think Mrs Puffin should remain here. I want her to. I want her to meet Victor.
HENRY. Are you mad?
ETHEL. You'll break Victor's heart. Poor, poor Victor, loving you as he does to have his—his—(*dramatically*) cup of happiness dashed from his lips by this woman. (*She weeps*)
PAMELA. Oh, Jacky, please be careful.
JACKY. I am being careful.
HENRY. You are not. You are being misled by a lot of superstititious nonsense. (*He moves to* R *of Mrs Puffin*) Mrs Puffin, will you please go.
MRS PUFFIN. I'd like to oblige, sir, but I can't, see? It never 'appened that way.

(*The front door bell rings*)

There! That's the Parkers. Now, what 'appens?
HENRY. You tell us.
ETHEL (*moving behind the sofa; frantically*) Get her out the back way. Henry, Henry—do something.

(NICHOLAS *moves up* C *and looks off*)

NICHOLAS. Too late, Annie's letting them in. (*He moves up* R)
MRS PUFFIN. The study! I get shoved in there. Quick, get hold of me! (*She pulls up her coat collar*)
HENRY. Into the study. (*He grasps Mrs Puffin by her coat collar and almost drags her to the door down* R) Not a word from you. Keep in there.
MRS PUFFIN. I told you I'd come in 'ere sometime. 'Ere's where I see that ruddy clock again.

(MRS PUFFIN *exits down* R)

HENRY (*crossing to* C) Not a word, do you understand, from anybody.
JACKY. Sorry, Daddy, I shall use my own discretion.

(ANNIE *enters up* C *and stands aside.* PAMELA *moves down* R)

ANNIE (*announcing*) Mr Stephen and Mr Victor Parker.

(STEPHEN *and* VICTOR PARKER *enter up* C. STEPHEN *is a self-made man, and looks it. Business is his whole life, and in that he brooks no interference. He carries a despatch case.* VICTOR *is shorter than Stephen, of rather solid build, and he gazes on the world through horn-rimmed glasses, in a rather shy and diffident manner. He is altogether a more likeable person than his father.*)

ANNIE *exits up* C)

STEPHEN. Ah, good evening, Fordyce—Mrs Fordyce. (*He shakes hands with Henry and Ethel*) Pamela, Jacqueline, Nicholas. (*He nods to each of them in turn*)

(*The Fordyce family, with the exception of* JACKY *and* NICHOLAS, *are all slightly on edge, with frequent glances at the study door.* ETHEL *has made a strenuous effort to recover, and* HENRY *is full of false heartiness*)

HENRY (*very heartily*) Sit down everybody. Hullo, Parker, glad to see you.
ETHEL. I'm so glad you both came.
JACKY ⎫ ⎧ Hullo.
PAMELA ⎬ (*together*) ⎨ Good evening, Mr Parker.
NICHOLAS ⎭ ⎩ Evening, sir.
VICTOR. Good evening, everyone. (*He moves to Jacky*) Hullo, Jacky. (*He kisses her very primly*)
JACKY. Hullo, Victor.

HENRY. Come and sit down, Stephen. Glad to see you. (*He ushers Stephen to the easy chair* LC)
ETHEL (*sitting on the sofa, at the right end of it*) Sit here, Victor. (*She pats the seat beside her*)

(VICTOR *sits* C *of the sofa.* JACKY *sits* L *of Victor on the sofa.* STEPHEN *sits in the easy chair* LC *and puts his case on the floor beside the chair.* HENRY *moves to the fireplace*)

STEPHEN. Well, Jacqueline, how are the preparations getting along for the great day?
JACKY. As a matter of fact, I . . .
HENRY (*heartily and hastily*) They are going on well, Parker, old man. Extremely well, in fact.
ETHEL. Oh, yes, and the wedding dress looks lovely.
STEPHEN. Glad to hear it. Must see that everything goes off all right. Wouldn't do to have any slips, would it, eh?
HENRY. No, no, no! Definitely not. God forbid! Quite unthinkable. Look—er—look, how about a drink? Nicholas, get the drinks.

(NICHOLAS *crosses to the table up* L *and pours the drinks*)

ETHEL. Yes, yes, Nicholas, get the drinks. (*She fans herself with her handkerchief*) Hasn't it been terribly cold today?
STEPHEN. Cold? I thought it was very warm for the time of the year. According to tonight's paper it's the warmest December day for over ten years.
ETHEL. Oh, dear, is it really?
STEPHEN. Not catching a cold, are you? Can't have the bride's mother with a bad cold before the wedding, can we, Victor?
VICTOR. Oh, no. You haven't the early symptoms, have you, Mrs Fordyce? I am most susceptible to colds.
ETHEL. No, Victor, of course not. No. I just thought—I mean—it's December and . . . Oh, Nicholas, haven't you got those drinks yet?
NICHOLAS. Just coming.
STEPHEN. I suppose you are getting very excited, Jacqueline?
JACKY. Well, to be perfectly honest . . .

(NICHOLAS *picks up the tray of drinks and moves* C)

HENRY (*crossing to* C) Ah, the drinks at last. (*He takes a glass from the tray and hands it to Stephen*) Whisky for you, Stephen, old man. He knows your taste. (*He fetches the soda syphon from the table up* C *and takes it to Stephen*) Say when. (*He splashes soda into Stephen's glass*)

(NICHOLAS *passes round with the drinks, finishing with Pamela, down* R, *then he puts the tray on the table* R)

(*He crosses to Victor*) How about you, Victor?

VICTOR. Oh, very weak for me.

HENRY (*splashing soda into Victor's glass*) Ah, then you will be a long time saying "When". (*He moves behind the sofa*)

STEPHEN. But in a very short time saying "I will".

HENRY. What's that? Oh, yes! (*He laughs heartily. Frantically, in a whisper*) Laugh, Mother. (*He prods Jacky*)

(*The Fordyce family laugh immoderately at this small joke*)

STEPHEN. Here's to the happy pair.

(HENRY *crosses up* L, *puts down the syphon and collects his own drink*)

May the arrangements continue to run smoothly.

VICTOR. Thank you, Father. I am sure they will.

(HENRY *moves* C)

JACKY. I would like to say . . .

(HENRY *splutters and coughs over his drink*)

ETHEL (*hastily*) Hasn't it been cold today? I mean—warm. Have another drink, Mr Parker.

STEPHEN. Not at the moment, thank you. Are you *sure* you haven't got a cold coming?

ETHEL. No, really—of course not.

VICTOR. You should eat oranges, you know. People who eat oranges freely are immune from colds and chills.

NICHOLAS. Have an orange, Mother, do. (*He picks up a bowl of oranges from the table up* R *and moves to* L *of the sofa*) We have plenty here.

STEPHEN. I'm not sure about oranges. Hot bath last thing at night with a hot whisky and lemon and two aspirins. Finest thing in the world.

ETHEL. Oh, yes—yes . . .

STEPHEN. I should have it tonight. If you felt cold today, we mustn't take any chances, you know. Too near the wedding. Can't have you give Jacqueline a cold, can we?

ETHEL. No, no, certainly not. I will—I mean, I'll have the whisky . . .

STEPHEN. D'you feel all right, Jacqueline?

JACKY. Oh, yes, I feel fine, but . . .

NICHOLAS (*offering the bowl to Jacky*) Suck an orange just in case, dear.

JACKY. No, thank you.

STEPHEN (*to Henry*) How about you, Fordyce? Do you feel all right?

NICHOLAS (*offering the bowl to Henry*) Perhaps you'd like an orange, Father?

HENRY. No, no, I feel fine. Never felt better.

ACT II GOOD NIGHT MRS PUFFIN 37

STEPHEN. Good! Treacherous things, colds.
HENRY. Oh, very. Couldn't agree with you more. The amount of man power wasted each year through colds . . .
STEPHEN. Amounts to millions, millions. All because people will not take simple precautions.
NICHOLAS (*offering the bowl to Stephen*) Are you sure you won't have an orange, Mr Parker?
HENRY. Put those blood-oranges down, Nicholas. We're all drinking.

(NICHOLAS *replaces the bowl on the table up* R)

VICTOR. How is your bridesmaid's frock looking, Pamela?
PAMELA. Oh, lovely, thank you, Victor.
STEPHEN. We mustn't forget the chief bridesmaid, must we?
ETHEL. No, certainly not. I suppose I'll be losing my other little girl, soon.

(PAMELA *sits on the right arm of the sofa*)

NICHOLAS. Never mind, dear; you've still got your little boy.
VICTOR. Why, have you . . .? I mean—I thought Pamela . . . She isn't engaged.
PAMELA. No, of course not. That's only mother's way.
JACKY. Perhaps if I could say . . .
HENRY (*desperately*) Millions, it must be millions. Everywhere.

(*There is a pause as the others all look at Henry*)

STEPHEN. What on earth are you talking about, Henry?
HENRY. Colds.
STEPHEN. Yes, but I thought we had settled that.
HENRY (*desperately*) And, do you know, I read once that Eskimos never catch cold. Extraordinary thing, that, isn't it? I mean, living where they do.
VICTOR. Blubber.
HENRY. Oh, yes—yes—blubber—most certainly.
NICHOLAS. But no oranges.
VICTOR. Oh, no, they don't have oranges there.
NICHOLAS. Really? I should hate to be an Eskimo. Fancy never knowing the joy of sucking an orange.
VICTOR. But what you never have you never miss.
HENRY. True, true, very true.

JACKY ⎫   ⎧ I think I ought to tell you that . . .
STEPHEN ⎬ (*together*) ⎨ Oh, by the way, Fordyce . . . I beg
        ⎭   your pardon, Jacqueline—you were
                         ⎩ saying?

JACKY. I was going to say . . .

(NICHOLAS *pulls Jacky's hair and sits on the left arm of the sofa*)

No, please. Please go on.

STEPHEN. Thank you. I was going to ask if you had received an acceptance from Sir William and Lady Francis?

ETHEL. Oh, yes, they are coming.

STEPHEN. Good! Good! Excellent business contact there, Henry.

HENRY. Oh, undoubtedly.

STEPHEN. And, by the way, I nearly forgot. A business representative will be coming here tonight. I hope you don't mind, but I want you to meet him. Perhaps you would invite him to the wedding, Mrs Fordyce; he will be here for a month.

ETHEL. Yes, of course.

HENRY. Delighted to meet him. Any friend of yours, Parker, friend of mine, y'know.

STEPHEN. Thank you, very kind of you, I'm sure. Well, this has been delightful, and now to business. (*He puts his glass on the table* LC *and picks up his case*) I have the deeds of the partnership here, Fordyce. Ah, I'm a happy man, Fordyce. Immediately after the wedding, when Jacqueline and Victor become one, "Parker and Son" and "Fordyce and Son" become "Parker, Fordyce and Sons". As I said to Victor tonight, a love marriage and a business marriage.

HENRY. Yes, yes, a great day. (*He looks frantically at Jacky*)

STEPHEN (*rising*) Well, shall we adjourn to your study?

HENRY (*moving down* C) Yes, yes, of course.

ETHEL (*gesturing with her head towards the study*) Henry!

HENRY. What, my dear? (*Loudly*) Oh, no—I mean—(*softly*) no.

STEPHEN. Why? Isn't it convenient? We went in there before.

HENRY. Well, it's warmer in here, yes, much warmer.

STEPHEN. But there is an electric fire there.

HENRY. Yes, oh yes—but we—well . . .

ETHEL. It's the decorators.

STEPHEN. The what?

HENRY. Yes, the decorators—in there—very messy.

(*The telephone rings.* PAMELA *rises and moves* R)

It's the telephone.

(*There is a pause*)

(*He moves to the telephone and lifts the receiver*) Oh, the phone, excuse me a moment. (*Into the telephone*) Hampstead five-nine-six-three . . . Yes, this is the Fordyce residence . . . What? . . . Who? . . . Your old woman? . . .

(MRS PUFFIN *enters down* R. *She has discarded her coat and wears an overlong crocheted silk jersey.* STEPHEN *puts his case on the floor* R *of the easy chair* LC *and moves down* L)

ACT II GOOD NIGHT MRS PUFFIN 39

Mrs Puffin (*moving to Henry*) All right, dearie, I'll answer 'im.

(Henry *swings round*)

(*She takes the receiver from Henry. To the Company in general*) 'E's a cantankerous old devil if I ain't there for 'is meal.

(Henry *backs up* c)

'Scuse me. (*To Henry*) Five minutes ago I knew this was going to 'appen, and I knew I answered it, so of course I 'ad to. (*Into the telephone*) 'Allo, Alf . . . What? . . . 'Course I'm 'ere . . . Well, pop round the corner for some fish and chips. You ain't bloody 'elpless, are yer? . . . (*To the others*) 'Scuse me, that slipped out. But old Alf's like a baby. (*Into the telephone*) I don't know 'ow long I'll be, Alf, but I was right. Dead right . . . Yers, uncanny, ain't it? . . . Fancy you remembering the name and address . . . Eh, what? . . . Now, shut your gob, Alfred Puffin, you know I feel it's my duty. 'Ave yer supper, get young Charlie to bed and see that 'e—(*she glances round at the others*) goes *before* this time, then you can pop off to the *Hit and Miss* until closing time . . . What? . . . 'Course I do. (*She replaces the receiver and turns to the others*) Silly ass! Do I still love 'im? 'E's all right, really, 'eart of gold but a bit abstroperous if 'e misses 'is grub. But 'e'll be all right in the pub. (*She sees Stephen and Victor*) Oooh, I say!

Stephen (*stupefied*) Who—who—is that?

Mrs Puffin (*moving to Henry*) 'Ere. (*She whispers*) Knew 'em at once. (*She moves* c)

(Nicholas *rises and moves up* R)

Stephen. Who is this woman?

Ethel. It's—it's our help.

Henry. She's just been cleaning up. Good night, Mrs Puffin. (*He moves up* L)

Mrs Puffin. Oh, I don't go.

Stephen. What on earth does she mean?

Jacky (*rising*) It's no good, Daddy. Mr Parker—Victor—let me introduce you to Mrs Puffin from Clapham Junction.

Victor (*rising and crossing to* R *of Mrs Puffin*) How do you do? (*He holds out his hand*)

Mrs Puffin (*shaking hands with Victor*) Very well, I'm sure.

Stephen. 'Evening. (*To Henry*) But what was she doing in your study?

Mrs Puffin. Waiting.

Stephen. Waiting? What for?

Mrs Puffin. Well, you see, when I first went in there I wasn't sure, but after about five minutes, I knew, and I waited for the phone to ring.

Stephen. You waited for the phone to ring?

Victor. Oh, you were expecting the call?

MRS PUFFIN. Not at first, but I gradually came up-to-date.

(STEPHEN *shrugs and turns away down* L)

NICHOLAS. You will find she takes a bit of getting used to at first, but after a time she will grow on you.

HENRY (*with great heartiness*) Well, Mrs Puffin, you have had your call, and we must not keep you. You must get back to your husband. We husbands don't like being kept waiting, do we? Good night, Mrs Puffin. (*To Ethel*) Say good night to Mrs Puffin, dear, she's just going.

JACKY (*moving to* R *of Victor*) Mrs Puffin says the wedding will not take place.

HENRY
ETHEL } (*together*) Jacky!

PAMELA. Oh, Jacky, how could you?

NICHOLAS (*moving behind the sofa*) Here we go!

JACKY. Well, I think Victor and his father should know.

STEPHEN. But what the devil has it got to do with Mrs Puffin?

HENRY. Nothing at all, old man, nothing at all. Just a stupid joke.

VICTOR. Is she forbidding the banns?

NICHOLAS. In a roundabout way, I suppose she is.

VICTOR. Oh, dear, why?

HENRY. I'm damned if I know.

JACKY. It's all very simple . . .

HENRY (*moving to the fireplace*) Simple? *Simple!*

JACKY. Yes, simple. It's a long story, but what it amounts to is this. Mrs Puffin had a dream, and in it she dreamt that Victor and I—don't—get—married.

STEPHEN. I never heard anything so damn silly in all my life. (*He sits in the easy chair down* L)

HENRY. That's exactly what I say, old man. I'm delighted to hear you echo my sentiments. (*He sits in the easy chair* LC)

STEPHEN. Absolutely ridiculous!

(MRS PUFFIN *moves down* LC, *sizes up Stephen rather belligerently then moves* C)

MRS PUFFIN. 'Ere, 'arf a mo! My dream ain't been so very ridiculous so far. (*She points to Henry*) You ask 'im—(*she points to Nicholas*) or for that matter—'im. (*She points to Pamela*) But you can't ask 'er 'cause nothing 'as 'appened to 'er—yet.

STEPHEN. Now what does she mean?

HENRY. Absolutely nothing, old man. Nothing at all.

ETHEL. Henry! How can you dismiss my best tea service as nothing at all?

STEPHEN (*exasperated*) What has Mrs Fordyce's tea service got to do with it?

MRS PUFFIN (*moving to* R *of Stephen; with relish*) Oh, it was chronic. Got smashed to smithereens. There wasn't 'arf a crash.
STEPHEN. Did you break it?
MRS PUFFIN. Who? Me? No. I wasn't even in the room.
HENRY. It was an accident, a pure accident. Annie tripped over the cat.
ETHEL. But she knew it was going to happen long before it did. If you had only listened . . .
HENRY. Oh, blast your tea service! Will you shut up about it. (*To Stephen*) Just a coincidence.
JACKY. There have been far too many coincidences.
MRS PUFFIN (*moving* C) *Not* coincidences, ducks, and my dream ain't yet been fulfilled.
STEPHEN. Do you mean to say you have been dreaming about me?
MRS PUFFIN. Oh, yes. (*She points to Victor*) And 'im.
STEPHEN. Damned sauce!
MRS PUFFIN (*moving to* R *of Stephen*) Damned sauce? What about me? I go to bed one night, say good night to Alf, turn over and go to sleep. Do I get a perfect night's rest? Not on your sweet Nelly. No. I dream about the lot of you. Am I complaining? With no thought of reward, and so far, no thanks, I give up my time and take the trouble to come round 'ere and 'elp you. To 'elp.
HENRY. Nobody's asking for your help.
MRS PUFFIN (*moving above the easy chair* LC) A pretty pickle you'd be in if I 'adn't come along this afternoon.
HENRY. We couldn't be in a worse pickle than we are now.
STEPHEN (*rising*) We are in no pickle at all. (*He crosses to* C) Henry, I am amazed at you. You are going to allow a perfect stranger to stop this wedding, to ruin the lives of my son and your daughter?
HENRY. No, no, certainly not, Parker, old man. I'm against it.
STEPHEN. So I should think. (*To Mrs Puffin*) It is obvious that your predictions are not welcome. We refuse to be dreamt about. Good night. (*He picks up his case and moves up* C) We will go over the deeds of partnership.

(HENRY *rises*)

MRS PUFFIN (*pulling Henry's coat tails*) 'Ave you got the papers, dear, because 'e ain't.
JACKY. What do you mean by that?
MRS PUFFIN. What I say, dear; 'e ain't got the papers.
STEPHEN (*turning*) Madam, are you suggesting that I am a liar?
MRS PUFFIN. Gawd bless your 'eart and soul, no, love. But you ain't got the papers.
STEPHEN. This is fantastic! Henry, I refuse to discuss any business while this person remains in the room—in the house.

VICTOR. Forgive me asking, Father, but have you got the papers?
STEPHEN. Of course I've got the papers.
NICHOLAS. Are you sure?
STEPHEN. Of course I am sure. Are you doubting my word, Nicholas? Fordyce, am I to be insulted in your house?
HENRY. Certainly not, Parker, old man. (*He crosses to Nicholas*) Nicholas, how dare you! You know Mr Parker well enough to know that when he says he has a thing, he has it.
NICHOLAS. But I know Mrs Puffin well enough to know that when she says somebody hasn't got a thing, they haven't.
HENRY. You evidently don't know Mr Parker.
NICHOLAS. He certainly doesn't know Mrs Puffin.
JACKY. This could be quite easily settled if Mr Parker would produce the papers.
STEPHEN. I will *not* produce the papers. I refuse to pander to this woman.
MRS PUFFIN. It's all right, dear. You will.
STEPHEN. At the proper time and place, yes. But before you —no. That is final. (*He sits C of the sofa, holding his case firmly across his knees*)
VICTOR. But what baffles me is why Jacky and I don't get married. I mean, all arrangements have been made.
MRS PUFFIN. Oh, it's not your fault, love. She's swep' off 'er feet. Swep'!
VICTOR. Good heavens! By whom?
MRS PUFFIN (*removing her scarf*) I'd better loosen meself, eh? Or I shan't feel the benefit. Do you know, I can't remember. (*She crosses and sits in the easy chair down* L)
STEPHEN. This is outrageous! Victor, are you going to be influenced by this nonsense?
VICTOR. Certainly not.
MRS PUFFIN. You can't 'elp it, dear, you're prawns in the 'ands of Fate.
NICHOLAS. You see what we are? Prawns in the hands of Fate.
STEPHEN. Pawns in the hands of this woman. Or is it a conspiracy? Look here, Henry, are you trying to wriggle out of this partnership?
HENRY (*moving to* L *of the sofa*) No, no, certainly not, Stephen, old man. You've no right to make a suggestion like that.
STEPHEN. I will make suggestions. All this is very suspicious.
ETHEL. Are you suggesting that we are in league with this woman?
PAMELA (*moving down* R) Oh, Mother, please keep calm.
ETHEL. I will not keep calm. Look what I've had to put up with today. This woman invades my house, smashes my tea service. Then Jacky brings her back—my own children turn against me . . . (*She weeps noisily*)

PAMELA. Oh, Mother, don't upset yourself. (*She sits on the right arm of the sofa*)

HENRY. Look here, Parker, I won't have you upsetting my wife.

STEPHEN. I did not upset your wife.

JACKY (*moving between Henry and Stephen*) Everything would have been quite all right if you had showed us those papers.

VICTOR (*moving to* L *of Jacky*) Really, Jacky, my father is not expected to open his despatch case at the request of any Tom, Dick or Harry. Be reasonable.

JACKY. Reasonable!

VICTOR. Yes, reasonable. It is not our fault that this lady has upset your family. (*He crosses down* L.)

(JACKY *moves to the fireplace*)

NICHOLAS. Jacky had every right to ask to see the papers.

STEPHEN. She had no right.

VICTOR. I quite agree.

HENRY. Now, look here, Parker, all Jacky suggested was . . .

STEPHEN. Are you telling me I should do what your daughter suggests?

(MRS PUFFIN *vainly tries to get a word in edgeways*)

ETHEL. Any gentleman would be glad to oblige a lady.

STEPHEN. Oh, now I'm not a gentleman. Let me tell you . . .

HENRY. If there is any telling to be done, tell me.

MRS PUFFIN (*raising her voice*) Excuse me, but in a little while we shall 'ear music.

HENRY. If anybody touches the piano or wireless, whistles or sings . . .

STEPHEN. Who the hell do you think wants to sing now?

HENRY. I don't know, but I'm proving that woman wrong once if I can.

ETHEL. You never proved her wrong over my tea service.

HENRY. To hell with your tea service! Are you on her side or on ours?

ETHEL. I don't know where I am.

STEPHEN. For once this evening I heartily agree with you. Now, look here, Fordyce, I am a patient man . . .

HENRY. You haven't shown much patience this evening. Of all the obstinate, pig-headed . . .

STEPHEN. Obstinate? Pig-headed? I'm damned glad we never signed the papers . . .

HENRY. If you ever had them.

(*Carol singers are heard off, singing* "Good King Wenceslas")

NICHOLAS. Music!

(HENRY *rushes to the window* R *and pulls the curtains open*)

HENRY (*shouting*) Go away! Go away!

(HENRY *turns from the window and rushes out up* C)

VICTOR (*crossing to Nicholas*) I say, that was most peculiar.

NICHOLAS. Not at all. Father doesn't approve of carol singers.

VICTOR. No, I meant the singing. I mean, it was music, wasn't it?

NICHOLAS. Of a sort, yes.

HENRY (*off; shouting*) Go away!

(*The singing ceases abruptly*)

JACKY (*moving to* R *of the easy chair* LC) Oh, Victor darling, now you see what I mean.

VICTOR (*crossing to Mrs Puffin*) Did you know this was going to happen?

MRS PUFFIN. Oh, yes, dearie.

VICTOR. How extraordinary.

NICHOLAS. Not to us; we're getting used to it.

JACKY. You see, darling, ever since Mrs Puffin arrived, things like that have been happening, so naturally I wanted you to know.

STEPHEN. To say that music will be heard, a week before Christmas, is neither miraculous nor prophetic, with carol singers on every doorstep. She would have been hard put to it to predict anything like that in July.

NICHOLAS. Not at all. If Mrs Puffin had predicted music on a quiet Sunday afternoon in July, the band of the Coldstream Guards would have marched up the road.

STEPHEN. Fiddlesticks!

VICTOR. Mrs Puffin, everything that is happening now, has already occurred in your dreams?

MRS PUFFIN. Yes; queer, ain't it? And I'm quite all right in other ways. Never 'ad a day's illness in my life. 'Course, I've 'ad the childish ailments, who 'asn't? But . . .

STEPHEN. This is preposterous! Utterly impossible!

VICTOR (*taking off his glasses and polishing them*) Oh, I don't know, Father. If you have ever read Dunne's *Experiment with Time*, and *The Serial Universe*, you will find that he advances the theory that frequently in dreams the future is revealed to us. (*To Mrs Puffin*) Don't you agree?

MRS PUFFIN. Oh, yes. Of course, I 'aven't read the books myself, I prefer a bit of romance, but . . . 'Ere, 'ave I been written about in books?

VICTOR. Well, not exactly *you*, Mrs Puffin.

MRS PUFFIN. I was going to say . . .

(HENRY *enters up* C)

STEPHEN. Look here, Victor, if you're going to be taken in by this nonsense, I'm not. In any case, I have a strong objection to my future being revealed to Mrs Puffin. For heaven's sake, let's have a breath of sanity.

MRS PUFFIN. 'Ere, are you suggesting I've only got 'arf me marbles?

HENRY. I agree with you entirely, old man.

STEPHEN. I never asked your opinion.

JACKY (*moving to* L *of Henry*) Oh, do stop this bickering. Mr Parker, you can very easily prove this all wrong by producing the papers.

STEPHEN. I have already said, Jacqueline . . .

JACKY. "For heaven's sake, let's have a breath of sanity". Those were your very words. (*She moves up* C)

HENRY. Exactly. (*With exaggerated bravura*) Stephen, old man, we are a couple of hard-headed business men. Are we to have our business ruined, our children's marriage upset, spoil a friendship built on the rock of—of . . .

MRS PUFFIN. Ages.

HENRY. Well, are we? You and I who spend our working days fighting competition, building up our business, are we to be beaten by a woman who dreams? I hold you in deep respect, Stephen, old man, and I said to myself this evening—"If anybody can beat this, Stephen Parker can".

NICHOLAS. And smiling, the boy fell dead!

ETHEL. Yes, Mr Parker, we look to you. She can't be right every time. (*To Mrs Puffin*) And I hope after this you will go.

HENRY. Exactly, Ethel. Produce the papers, Mrs Puffin will depart, and we will settle down and resume our interrupted evening. (*He sits on the right arm of the easy chair* LC)

VICTOR. I should be most interested, Father.

JACKY. Please, Mr Parker, please.

STEPHEN. Very well.

NICHOLAS (*to Mrs Puffin*) I've got my shirt on you, darling.

STEPHEN (*rising and holding up his despatch case*) Here is my despatch case.

(NICHOLAS *applauds loudly*)

PAMELA. Be quiet, Nick. This is serious.

NICHOLAS. Sorry, everyone.

STEPHEN (*sternly*) I should think so. This is no time to be frivolous. Very well, then. Here is my despatch case. In it is a large envelope containing the proposed deeds of partnership between Parker and Fordyce. I received these deeds two days ago, placed them in this envelope, and put them in my safe at the office, personally. This evening, my secretary, Miss Adams—

VICTOR. A most capable woman.

(STEPHEN *gives Victor a look.* VICTOR *wilts*)

STEPHEN. —gave the envelope to me at my request, and I placed it in this case. (*To Mrs Puffin*) Now you, madam, assert the papers are not here.
MRS PUFFIN (*who has been listening with awe*) Ain't 'e got a lovely flow of words? They just come out like oil.
STEPHEN (*pompously*) Did you, or did you not, say the papers were not here?
MRS PUFFIN. Yes, I did.
STEPHEN. Very well, then. (*He pulls back his cuffs rather like a conjuror about to perform a trick*)

(*There is a deathly silence as the others watch*)

(*He opens his case, extracts a large white envelope, turns the case upside down and shakes it to show that it is empty, hands the envelope to Nicholas, turns and puts the case on the table up* R) Open it.

(NICHOLAS *takes the envelope, glances at Mrs Puffin, tears it open and pulls out a sheaf of papers*)

NICHOLAS (*solemnly reading*) "Five pounds each way 'Jolly Roger' " . . .
STEPHEN. What! What did you say?
NICHOLAS (*patiently*) I said, "Five pounds each . . ."
STEPHEN (*snatching the papers*) Let me see that! (*He glances at the papers and flings them furiously to the floor*) That damned fool Miss Adams . . .
ETHEL. Mr Parker, what has happened?
STEPHEN. My damned secretary gave me the wrong envelope. (*He sits* L *of Ethel on the sofa*)
NICHOLAS. Up the Puffins!
ETHEL (*wailing*) Now we are back where we started.
MRS PUFFIN (*rising*) I knew that was going to 'appen.
STEPHEN. Oh, you did, did you?
MRS PUFFIN (*crossing to Stephen*) Yes, I told you, you Turk! Now, I don't want to be a nuisance . . .
HENRY (*rising and moving to* L *of Mrs Puffin*) We can see that.
MRS PUFFIN. Well, I don't. I'm only trying to 'elp. Look at you. Gone to all the expense of this wedding which ain't going to take place.
ETHEL (*wailing*) Oh, you've ruined everything. What will all the neighbours say? The guests? And we'll have to return all the presents. Oh, oh.

(MRS PUFFIN *whispers to* JACKY *who points up* R. MRS PUFFIN *goes to the table up* R *and takes a bottle of smelling-salts from Ethel's handbag*)

Henry, don't just stand there—do something.

(MRS PUFFIN *moves behind the sofa*)

Oh, this has given me one of my heads—where are my smelling salts?

(Mrs Puffin *leans over the back of the sofa and hands the bottle to Ethel*)

Mrs Puffin. They're already 'ere, dear. (*To the others*) I knew she'd want them. (*She moves below the armchair* LC)

(Jacky *moves behind the sofa*)

Henry. Is there anything you don't know?
Mrs Puffin. I still can't remember that other bloke's name or what 'e looks like. Oh, dear, you must think me a silly fool.
Stephen. What fellow is this?
Mrs Puffin. I told you. The bloke who sweeps Miss Jacqueline off her feet. Give meself clergyman's throat talking to you.
Stephen. Victor, that's your affair.
Mrs Puffin. I'm real sorry for 'im. (*She turns to Victor*) I am really, ducks, but what can I do? It's Fate.
Stephen (*rising*) Now I'll tell you something else about Fate. If you think I'm going to have my son jilted and made to look a fool, you're wrong. Nobody ever made a fool of the Parkers.
Mrs Puffin (*sitting in the easy chair* LC) Nature 'ad a jolly good try.
Stephen. And I tell you, Fordyce, if I'm made to look a fool, the partnership is off. *Off!* (*He moves up* C)

(Jacky *moves down* R)

Henry. Just a minute, Parker, old man, just a minute. There is one thing we have not considered. Victor, forget Mrs Puffin and her talk about Fate. As man to man, I want to ask you a question.
Victor. Yes, Mr Fordyce?
Henry. Do you love Jacky?
Victor (*looking steadily at Jacky*) Yes, Mr Fordyce.
Henry. I knew it! I knew it! Jacky, my dear, it's foolish to ask—but do you love Victor?
Jacky (*looking at Victor; quietly*) Yes, I do.

(Henry *sits on the left arm of the sofa and triumphantly snaps his fingers*)

Henry. There, Mrs Puffin, you can't fight love.
Mrs Puffin (*plaintively*) I ain't fighting anything, I was only trying to 'elp. I still can't understand it, something's gorn wrong somewhere, I ain't never been wrong before.
Nicholas. Cheer up, Mrs Puffin. Here, come and have a drop of "mother's ruin" before you go. (*He crosses to the table up* L)
Stephen (*moving to Henry*) I congratulate you, Fordyce. (*He*

crosses to Victor) My dear Victor, my dear Jacqueline, I am exceedingly happy.

ETHEL (*rising*) Oh, darlings! (*She kisses Jacky*)

(HENRY *goes to Ethel. There is a babble of talk and general congratulations.* NICHOLAS *takes a glass of gin to Mrs Puffin and goes to the fireplace.*

ANNIE *enters up* C *and stands to one side*)

ANNIE (*announcing*) Mr Roger Vincent.

(ROGER VINCENT *enters up* C. *He is a good-looking young man with a pleasant smile*)

STEPHEN. Ah, hullo.

(ROGER *moves down* C. *At the same time* MRS PUFFIN *raises her glass to her lips and sees him*)

MRS PUFFIN (*rising*) My Gawd, it's 'im!

JACKY *moves slowly towards Roger and offers him her hand as—*

the CURTAIN *falls*

ACT III

SCENE—*The same. Three days later. Evening.*
When the CURTAIN *rises, it is about seven-thirty. The room is lit by the table-lamps and the glow of the fire.* JACKY *and* ROGER, *in evening dress, are locked in an embrace* C, *on the same spot as they were at the end of the previous Act. There is a long kiss.*

JACKY. Darling, it's been a lifetime.
ROGER. Longer than that. Four hours.
JACKY. Two lifetimes, then.

(*There is another kiss, but after a moment, a door bangs upstairs.* ROGER *breaks away down* L)

ROGER. Father, mother, sister, brother?
JACKY. They are all upstairs dressing. I got down early especially.
ROGER. I got here early especially.
JACKY. And now, Mr Vincent, may I offer you a cocktail? (*She moves to the table up* L)
ROGER (*moving to* L *of Jacky*) Certainly, Miss Fordyce.

(JACKY *pours two cocktails from a shaker*)

You grow lovelier every day, and today you look like tomorrow.
JACKY (*handing him a drink*) Thank you, darling, and where did you hear that?
ROGER. Well, I got it from some T.V. programme, but give me time, and I'll think up some good ones, too.
JACKY. I'm sure you will. (*She raises her glass*) To . . .?
ROGER (*raising his glass*) Us.

(*They drink*)

(*He crosses to the coffee-table*) Look, Jacky, I feel like a heel.
JACKY. So do I.
ROGER. If Victor weren't such a darn nice guy—you see, I like him. I wish I didn't. (*He puts his glass on the coffee-table*)
JACKY (*crossing to* L *of Roger*) I wish I weren't so awfully fond of him. Oh, Roger, I never believed in love at first sight.
ROGER. Neither did I. (*He takes Jacky's glass, puts it on the coffee-table, kisses her, then jerks his head upwards*) Do they know?
JACKY (*in a small voice*) No.
ROGER. I felt terrible yesterday when Victor invited me to lunch and I found you with him. (*He crosses to the fireplace*)
JACKY. So did I. (*She moves to the easy chair* LC) Oh, Roger, I'm a terrible coward. Mrs Puffin, Mrs Puffin, why didn't you dream some more? (*She sinks into the easy chair* LC)

ROGER. I wish I had had time to really meet that old girl. But she was bustled out so soon after I first arrived that I didn't have a chance.

JACKY. Poor Mrs Puffin hardly had time to finish her gin.

ROGER (*sitting on the left arm of Jacky's chair*) I'd buy her a dozen cases if she'd only dream a happy ending about us. Can't she do it to order?

JACKY. No, it just happens.

ROGER. But, listen, honey, she said you would be swept off your feet by someone from over the water.

JACKY. And I have been. (*She turns and nestles in his arms*)

ROGER. I haven't reached earth yet. But she also said the wedding wouldn't take place. But it is taking place. Hell! Why is Victor such a nice guy? Why can't I hate him?

JACKY. Because he is Victor—and nice. I can't hurt him. Roger, he loves me. If Victor weren't so . . . Oh, Roger, try to understand. If the wedding was in six months' time, it would be different.

ROGER. Listen, couldn't I speak to Victor?

JACKY. No, Roger, you couldn't.

ROGER. But as he's such a nice guy he'd understand.

JACKY. Would father, or Mr Parker? Father's set on the partnership, he needs it. Fordyce and Son aren't too flourishing. If there is no wedding, there will be a scandal. And with Mr Parker—a scandal—no partnership.

(ROGER *kisses her*)

ROGER (*sighing*) We need a miracle to help us. The amazing thing about miracles is, they sometimes happen. That's not original, either.

JACKY. I know, but it's very comforting. (*She rises and crosses to the coffee-table. In a small voice*) Roger, talk about something else. Anything. I think I'm going to cry.

ROGER (*rising and moving above the easy chair* LC) Jacky darling, what have I done?

JACKY. Please! Please talk about something else.

ROGER. Hell, I can't think of a darn thing. Oh, Jacky, I love you.

JACKY (*sitting on the coffee-table and sniffing*) You're a great help. That will make me worse.

ROGER. Oh, gee! Why was I invited tonight?

JACKY. You can thank Nicky for that. He told mother you were a good bridge player.

ROGER. If your mother gets me for a bridge partner, this romance is really on the rocks.

JACKY. And after all, you are the American Representative of Parker and Son.

ROGER (*moving and kneeling beside Jacky*) Couldn't we just slip off somewhere?
JACKY. No, darling, not a chance. Darling Roger.
ROGER. Darling Jacky.

(*They kiss briefly*)

JACKY (*picking up her glass*) Cheers! Nicky mixed these.

(*The front door bell rings*)

I expect that's Victor and his father.
ROGER (*rising*) Then make mine a double. (*He picks up his glass and crosses to the table up* L)
JACKY (*rising and moving down* R) Darling! The lights!

(ROGER *hastily switches on the wall-brackets then returns to the table up* L.
PAMELA *and* VICTOR *enter up* C)

PAMELA. Hullo, Roger, I never heard you arrive.
ROGER. Hullo, Pam. Have a drink?
VICTOR. Good evening, Roger.
ROGER. Hullo, Victor. How are you? (*He pours the drinks*)
VICTOR. Fine, thanks. (*He goes to Jacky and kisses her chastely*) Hullo, darling.
JACKY. Hullo, Victor. Where is your father?
VICTOR. He has been delayed, but he will only be a few minutes late. He asked me to make his apologies; he is usually so punctual. I am, too.
JACKY. I know. Even my habit of being late doesn't alter you, darling.

(PAMELA *moves to the table up* L, *picks up two drinks and gives one to Victor*. ROGER *refills his own and Jacky's glasses*)

PAMELA. You see, Victor, if you would only be late, Jacky would be on time.
VICTOR. Oh, I couldn't do that.
JACKY. I'll have to try and change my ways.
VICTOR. Oh, don't do that. I don't mind waiting. Really.
JACKY (*with a look at Roger*) You are very sweet, Victor.

(ROGER *crosses and hands Jacky her drink*)

ROGER (*raising his glass*) Well, cheers!
JACKY
VICTOR   } (*together*) Cheers!
PAMELA

(*They drink*)

VICTOR. Have you seen the wedding presents, Roger?
ROGER. No—I—er—haven't.

VICTOR. They are in the study.
ROGER. Oh, good.
VICTOR. Yes, we've received some very nice toast racks, among other things. Seven, I think.
JACKY. No, eight. Miriam and Charles have sent another.
VICTOR. Oh, how nice of them. Just what we wanted, and I do hate toast.
ROGER. May I see the presents?
JACKY (*to Victor*) Do you mind?
VICTOR. Of course not. Go ahead.
ROGER. Thank you.

(JACKY *and* ROGER *exit down* R. *There is a long pause.* VICTOR *drinks and nearly chokes*)

VICTOR (*holding up his glass*) Very refreshing.
PAMELA. Yes, a Nicholas special. Have another?
VICTOR. No, thank you. I never have more than one. (*He sits on the sofa, then rises hurriedly*) I'm awfully sorry. After you.

(PAMELA *sits on the sofa.* VICTOR *sits* R *of Pamela on the sofa. There is a pause*)

PAMELA
VICTOR } (*together*) Well, it won't be long now!

PAMELA
VICTOR } (*together*) No, it won't!

(*There is a pause*)

VICTOR. I hope I can make Jacky happy. (*He puts his glass on the coffee-table*)
PAMELA (*putting her glass on the coffee-table*) Why ever not?
VICTOR (*polishing his glasses; slowly*) Oh, I don't know. I just wondered.
PAMELA. Have you any need to wonder?
VICTOR. I'm afraid I'm rather a dull sort of chap.
PAMELA. No, Victor.
VICTOR. I am, and Jacky is so full of life. You know what I mean. And I like a book, slippers and a fire. Rather a dull chap, I mean, not lively like she is. In fact, I would go so far as to say stodgy. I can't make jokes—(*hastily*) though I can sometimes see one. I sometimes wonder what she sees in me.
PAMELA (*softly*) Someone very nice, very kind and dependable, a shoulder to lean on.

(VICTOR *gazes at her*)

Someone that, whatever happens, is there, always.
VICTOR. Is that what you see?
PAMELA. I do.

VICTOR. I never thought that—I wonder that no fellow has —ever . . .
PAMELA. Has what?
VICTOR. I just thought that . . .

(NICHOLAS *enters up* C. *He is in dinner clothes.* PAMELA *rises*)

NICHOLAS. Thank God somebody is entertaining the guests. Hullo, Victor. Aren't we bad-mannered? The trouble with Fordyce Castle is, too many Fordyces and not enough bathrooms. Have you sampled the Nicholas Deadly Nightshade yet?
VICTOR (*rising*) Good evening, Nicholas. Yes, it's very nice.
NICHOLAS. How many have you had?
VICTOR. One.
NICHOLAS (*moving to the table up* L.) You need more than that.

(VICTOR *picks up his glass and crosses to* NICHOLAS)

Confidentially, old boy, they are delayed action. I want to try them on father. (*He refills Victor's glass and pours a drink for himself*)

(VICTOR *moves to the fireplace*)

Come on, Pam, have another.

(PAMELA *picks up her glass and crosses to* NICHOLAS *who refills it.*
JACKY *and* ROGER *enter down* R. *They still have their glasses.* JACKY *stands up* L *of the sofa.* ROGER *stands down* R *of the sofa.* PAMELA *joins Victor at the fireplace*)

Hullo, Roger. Have you had a Nicholas Deadly Nightshade?
ROGER. I've had two.
NICHOLAS. Is that all?
PAMELA. Delayed action. Very potent.
ROGER. No effect after two.
NICHOLAS (*picking up the shaker and crossing behind the sofa*) Wait until the third, old boy— (*he stands between Jacky and Roger*) when the most amazing things begin to happen. (*He refills Roger's glass*) Here you are. You, too, Jacky?
JACKY. If you like.

(NICHOLAS *refills Jacky's glass*)

NICHOLAS. What have you two been up to?
ROGER. We've been in the study looking at the wedding presents.
NICHOLAS. That must have been very stimulating. (*He crosses to the table up* L *and replaces the shaker*) Did you see that awful pot thing from our Aunt Maud? Every time one of the Fordyce clan gets married, Aunt Maud coughs up a pot. I don't know where she finds them.
JACKY. It's a table centre. (*She moves and sits on the sofa, at the right end of it*)

NICHOLAS *(picking up his drink and moving* LC) Is it? Well, live and learn. Anyhow, that's one reason why I'm a confirmed bachelor. The very thought of Aunt Maud hugging a pot, waiting to bung it at me, is enough to make me steer clear of marriage. A table centre, is it? Well, well!
VICTOR. I thought it was very nice.
NICHOLAS *(staring at Victor)* You do need another drink.

(HENRY *and* ETHEL *enter up* C. *They are in evening dress.* NICHOLAS *moves to the table up* L *and pours drinks for Henry and Ethel)*

HENRY. Good evening, everyone.
ETHEL *(crossing and sitting* L *of Jacky on the sofa)* I'm so sorry we are late.
HENRY *(moving* C) Yes, Nicholas—*(with meaning)* we have only one bathroom.
NICHOLAS. My very words to Roger. *(He picks up the drinks and moves to Henry)* Here, have a drink.
HENRY *(taking the drink)* Thanks.

(NICHOLAS *takes a drink to Ethel then returns up* L)

Good evening, Roger. Glad you were able to come.
ROGER. Nice of you to ask me, sir.
ETHEL. How are you, Roger?
ROGER. Fine, thanks. And you?
ETHEL. Well, a little excited, you know.
ROGER. I guess so.
HENRY. Why, Victor, where is your father?
VICTOR. He has been delayed. He should be here shortly.
HENRY. Ah, busy man, your father, very busy man. Well, Roger, what do you think of London?
ROGER *(looking at Jacky)* Oh, beautiful, sir. Oh! London! Well, I've been here before, a few years ago. Air Force.
HENRY. Really?
ROGER. Yes. I feel as though I've come home.
ETHEL. Oh, how nice. We are always pleased to welcome one of our Allies.
NICHOLAS. Nobly said, Mother. Mother was in the W.V.S. during the war and still feels personally responsible for all the Forces.

(The front door bell rings. The Fordyce family react)

VICTOR *(after a pause)* I think you'll find that's father.
HENRY. I hope.
VICTOR. Father is like me. He feels very keenly about punctuality.
HENRY. No need to bother here, my boy.
ETHEL. No. I always say we want everyone to feel at home.

ACT III GOOD NIGHT MRS PUFFIN 55

NICHOLAS. So park your feet on the mantelpiece any time.

(ANNIE *enters up* C *and stands aside.* HENRY *moves hastily to Annie*)

HENRY. Who is it, Annie?
ANNIE. Mr Stephen Parker.

(STEPHEN *enters hurriedly up* C. *He is in evening dress.*
ANNIE *exits up* C)

STEPHEN (*moving to* R *of Henry*) Henry, Mrs Fordyce, I'm most terribly sorry.

(NICHOLAS *takes a drink to Stephen*)

HENRY. You're a little out of breath, old man.
STEPHEN. Just puffing a bit. (*He realizes what he has said and hastily carries on*) Sir William Francis telephoned just as I was leaving. Big thing there, Fordyce. I think I can promise that Parker and Fordyce will start off with a bang.
HENRY. Delighted to hear it, Stephen, old man.
STEPHEN. How are you, Mrs Fordyce? Roger?
ROGER. Good evening, sir.
STEPHEN (*to Ethel*) My word, your husband will be kept very busy shortly.
ETHEL. I am sure he will, but Henry is a glutton for work.
STEPHEN. You, too, Nicholas.
NICHOLAS. That will be fun.

(ANNIE *enters up* C)

ANNIE. Dinner is served.

(ANNIE *exits up* C)

ETHEL (*rising*) Come along, everyone. (*She moves up* C)

(JACKY *rises. There is a general movement towards the door up* C)

STEPHEN (*to Jacky*) And how is the bride-to-be? Well, I hope?
JACKY. Yes, thank you.

(ETHEL, PAMELA, JACKY *and* NICHOLAS *exit up* C)

STEPHEN. That's right. My word, she looks prettier every day, doesn't she, Fordyce?
HENRY. Yes, rather.

(STEPHEN *and* HENRY *exit up* C)

ROGER. You can say that again! (*He realizes his slip and hastily swallows his drink*)

(VICTOR *moves to* L *of the steps up* C *and turns to ask Roger to go first with a gesture of his right hand.* ROGER *puts his glass into*

Victor's hand. VICTOR *turns away and puts the glass on the table up* L.

ROGER *exits hastily up* C.

VICTOR *turns and makes his gesture again, in vain, shrugs and follows Roger off. The* LIGHTS *dim to* BLACK-OUT *for a few moments to indicate the passing of about an hour. When the* LIGHTS *come up, the room is empty.*

ANNIE *enters up* C, *carrying a tray with coffee for eight. She puts the tray on the coffee-table, straightens a cushion or two and collects the dirty cocktail glasses*)

ETHEL *(off)* Now then, you men, don't be long.

(ETHEL, PAMELA *and* JACKY *enter up* C)

Thank you, Annie.

(ANNIE *exits up* C)

I do hope they are not too long. (*She crosses to the sofa and sits*) I do want a game of bridge.

PAMELA (*moving to* L *of the sofa*) I rather think it will be business.

ETHEL (*busy with the coffee*) Nonsense, they have business all day. (*She hands a cup of coffee to Pamela*)

(PAMELA *sits on the right arm of the easy chair* LC)

Well, I must say that was a most pleasant dinner. Bright intelligent conversation, and good food.

JACKY (*sitting* L *of Ethel on the sofa*) You sound like an advertisement for a seaside boarding-house.

ETHEL. You didn't have much to say, Jacky. Now I come to think of it, neither did Victor or Roger.

JACKY. We were all too busy listening to you, Mummy.

ETHEL. Someone has to keep the conversation going. I must say, with guests, one looks to one's children for *some* co-operation.

JACKY. But you said just now the dinner was full of light intelligent conversation.

ETHEL. Jacky, why will you twist my words? You know very well what I meant. You hardly said a word, and neither did Victor or Roger.

JACKY. Well, there was no need to. (*To Pamela*) Anything decent on the television?

ETHEL. Leave the television alone. You are changing the conversation. I don't like my conversations changed. Really, one would think I was . . .

JACKY. I'm sorry, Mother. I was a trifle quiet at dinner. I'm sorry, I just felt like it.

ETHEL. Why were Victor and Roger quiet, then?

JACKY. I don't know. You'd better ask them.

PAMELA. Oh, Mummy, it doesn't matter. Everything went off

very well. I enjoyed it. Have you finished your library book yet? I want to read it.

ETHEL. Now *you're* changing the conversation. Really! I sometimes wonder whether I can speak. (*To Jacky*) Have you been thinking about that Puffin woman?

PAMELA ⎱ (*together*) ⎰ (*Quickly*) No, of course not!
JACKY ⎰ ⎱ Of course not.

ETHEL. Well, it's very funny that you were all so quiet. That woman has had an evil influence. I had that tea service for ten years. Not a plate left whole.

PAMELA. Never mind. We will buy you another for Christmas.

(VICTOR *enters up* C)

Hullo, Victor.

VICTOR. I hope I'm not intruding?

ETHEL. Of course not. Come and have some coffee. (*She pours coffee for Victor*)

JACKY. Will the others be long?

VICTOR. I don't think so. (*He looks at his watch*) Is your clock right, Mrs Fordyce?

ETHEL. Yes, I think so. Why?

VICTOR. Nothing really, nothing. (*He crosses down* R) I just wondered.

PAMELA. You are a great one for time, aren't you, Victor?

VICTOR. Oh, yes. Time can be very important. Most important.

ETHEL. Well, time marches on. (*She holds out a cup of coffee to Victor*)

VICTOR. Yes, it does, doesn't it? (*He looks at his watch*)

JACKY. But not that quick, dear. Have you got an appointment?

VICTOR. No, no! (*He hurriedly takes the coffee*)

(NICHOLAS *and* ROGER *enter up* C. PAMELA *rises and moves above the easy chair* LC)

NICHOLAS (*moving to* L *of Ethel*) Two more coffees, please, Mother.

(ETHEL *pours coffee*)

Well, that was quite a blow-out.

ETHEL. Nicholas, it was a very nice dinner. (*She holds out a cup of coffee*)

NICHOLAS (*taking the coffee*) That's what I said.

ROGER (*moving to* L *of Nicholas*) It certainly was, Mrs Fordyce.

(NICHOLAS *hands the coffee to Roger*)

ETHEL. Thank you, Roger. Aren't the others coming? (*She hands Nicholas his coffee*)

NICHOLAS. Any moment now. (*To Roger*) Mother is a bridge

fiend. She and Culbertson play almost the same game, but he doesn't hold such an interesting inquest at the end of each hand.

ROGER. It's a very interesting game.

NICHOLAS. Played here, it's a matter of life or death. I told mother what an excellent player you were.

(ROGER *chokes over his coffee, crosses to the easy chair down* L *and sits*)

That was a very prompt answer. (*He moves behind the sofa*) I don't blame you.

ETHEL. Don't you take any notice of him, Roger.

(HENRY *and* STEPHEN *enter up* C. HENRY *moves to* L *of Ethel.* STEPHEN *follows to* L *of Henry*)

Coffee, Mr Parker? Henry? (*She pours coffee*)

STEPHEN. Thank you, Mrs Fordyce. (*To Henry*) So I said to him, "Do that, and you will regret it. Business", I said to him, "is business".

HENRY. Quite right, Parker, old man. And what did he say?

STEPHEN. Nothing.

HENRY. Ah, you had him there! I'm glad we are going to be partners instead of rivals.

STEPHEN. You would find me a tough nut to crack. (*He sits in the easy chair* LC)

HENRY (*crossing to the fireplace*) Did I ever tell you of that little affair I had with Collett and Palmer? They were . . .

ETHEL. Henry, really!

HENRY. What's that, dear?

PAMELA (*moving to the coffee-table*) Mummy wants to play bridge. (*She collects two cups of coffee, hands one to Stephen, the other to Henry, then moves up* LC)

ETHEL. Business, business, business. Always business. You see that Victor doesn't get like that, Jacky.

JACKY. I will, Mummy.

HENRY (*jovially*) Now you see what you're up against, Victor. Iron hand in the velvet glove. Put your foot down at the beginning my boy.

VICTOR. I'm not exactly the type for that, Mr Fordyce.

HENRY. You'll rue it, my boy, you'll rue it.

PAMELA. That's not very complimentary to Jacky.

JACKY. I don't mind. If Victor talks business, I shall listen.

VICTOR (*looking at his watch*) But I won't, I promise you.

ETHEL. Now, what about this game of bridge? (*She rises*)

(JACKY, ROGER *and* STEPHEN *rise*)

VICTOR. Has Mrs Puffin called again?

(*The others look in amazement at Victor*)

STEPHEN. What did you say, Victor?
VICTOR. I said, has Mrs Puffin called again?
STEPHEN. Dammit! That's what I thought you said.
JACKY. Why did you say that, Victor?
VICTOR. For no particular reason. I just wondered.
STEPHEN. But you can't say things for no particular reason. Don't you get that habit in business. Dangerous, eh, Fordyce?
HENRY. Yes, by Jove, it is!
VICTOR. All I meant was, she struck me as a woman of very strong convictions, and, right or wrong, she would abide by them. That's all.
ETHEL. Well, she's not going to have her convictions here any more.
STEPHEN. That was a damned tactless remark to make, Victor, damned tactless. Especially here. 'Pon my word,. Victor!
HENRY. Oh, that's all right, Parker, old man. We have forgotten the old crank.
ETHEL. Now, are we going to play . . .?

(*The front door bell rings. There is general reaction*)

Now, I wonder who that can be? Just as we were going to play. Never mind, we will set up the tables. Pam, Nicholas, get the tables from the study.

NICHOLAS. Come on, Pam. Bridge it is. (*He moves to the door down* R)

(PAMELA *crosses to Nicholas.*
  ANNIE *enters up* C)

ANNIE. Please, sir.
HENRY. Yes, Annie?
ANNIE. It's that Mrs Puffin again, sir.

(*There is general reaction.* VICTOR *moves up* R)

HENRY. No!
ANNIE. Yes, sir, it is.
ETHEL. Send her away! Send her away!
ANNIE. I tried, madam. I said you weren't in. Then she said you had Mr Stephen and Victor Parker here and Mr Vincent.
HENRY. What did you say?
ANNIE. Nothing, sir. I was flabbergasted. So I thought I'd best come in here and tell you.
ETHEL. Now you have come in and told us, go out and tell her that we don't want to see her. The idea!
HENRY. Exactly! The idea!
STEPHEN. I agree entirely, Henry.
NICHOLAS. Poor old Mrs Puffin, all the way from Clapham Junction.

HENRY (*crossing to* L *of the sofa*) I don't care if she came all the way from Nether Wallop, she can go back there.
JACKY. Nevertheless, it's very strange how she knew we were all here tonight.
HENRY. That's neither here nor there.
JACKY. All the same, she knew.

(VICTOR *crosses up* LC)

HENRY. She knew nothing. I trust you are not suggesting we should ask her in, because I warn you, Jacky . . .

(JACKY *looks at Victor, then at Roger*)

JACKY. No, Daddy, I'm *not*.
HENRY. I'm very glad to hear it. Annie, go and tell . . .
VICTOR (*moving to* L *of Henry*) I should like to see Mrs Puffin.

(*The others stare at Victor*)

STEPHEN. What?
VICTOR. I said, I should like to see Mrs Puffin.
STEPHEN. What the devil's come over you tonight? First you practically wish the damn woman on us, and now when she turns up, you want to see her.
HENRY. I must say, Victor, it's unwise. Most unwise. (*He moves up* C)
JACKY. Why do you want to see her, Victor?

(VICTOR, *as usual when concentrating, polishes his glasses*)

VICTOR. I can't explain, Jacky, really. But from what you have told me and what I have seen, I think she has a great gift. A great gift. You see, in the theory of Serialism . . .
STEPHEN. What the blazes are you talking about now?
VICTOR. I was just saying that I think we ought to see her. After all, it affects Jacky and me, and if nobody else sees her, I think we ought to.
JACKY. Do you really mean that, Victor?
VICTOR. Yes, I do. Don't you agree, Jacky?
JACKY. But, Victor—you know what she said?
VICTOR. Oh, yes.
STEPHEN. He *is* mad.
JACKY. All right, Victor.
VICTOR. I knew you would see my point.
STEPHEN (*crossing down* L) Now I know you're mad. That damn woman may have dreamt something else about us. I refuse to have my private life dreamt about by a perfect stranger. It's not decent.
VICTOR (*moving to* R *of the easy chair* LC) So you believe in her?
STEPHEN. What? Don't talk nonsense.
VICTOR. I think you do.

ACT III   GOOD NIGHT MRS PUFFIN   61

NICHOLAS. Mrs Puffin must be getting cold.
STEPHEN. She can freeze for all I care.
JACKY. Well, Daddy?
HENRY (*moving between Jacky and Victor*) Now, listen to me, Jacky—you, too, Victor. This woman . . .
ETHEL. Has a most unsettling influence. Jacky, you know how she unsettled me last time. I was thoroughly ill the next day. Wasn't I, Henry?
HENRY. Oh, yes, dreadful, dreadful.
JACKY. All right, Victor.
VICTOR. Thank you, Jacky.
STEPHEN. I've finished, d'you hear? Finished! (*He moves to the fireplace*)
HENRY. I must say I agree, Stephen, old man. I am sorry, Victor, we won't have her. (*He moves up* RC) Think of the consequences.
JACKY. In that case we will go out to her. Come on, Victor. (*She moves up* C)
VICTOR. You, too, Roger? (*He moves up* C)
ROGER (*moving up* C) I'm with you.
NICHOLAS (*moving up* C) I'm coming, too. She may have dreamt up something particularly juicy about me.
PAMELA (*moving up* C) I'm coming, too.
JACKY (*turning at the door*) I wonder what she will say this time?
ETHEL. Henry, stop them! Oh, Victor, how could you?
VICTOR. I really am sorry, Mrs Fordyce, but I do feel that . . .
HENRY (*crossing to Stephen*) Parker—I . . .
STEPHEN. I've had my say. (*He sits in the easy chair down* L)
HENRY. Oh, dammit, bring her in and it's on your own heads.
ETHEL. If she comes in, I go to bed.
NICHOLAS. Good night, Mother.
ETHEL. Well, I . . . Oh! (*She sits on the sofa*)
JACKY. Bring Mrs Puffin in, Annie.
ANNIE. Yes, miss.

(ANNIE *exits up* C)

NICHOLAS. Let us make ourselves comfortable, preparing for some more startling revelations. I'm glad she dreams of the future, not the past. (*He moves behind the sofa*)

(PAMELA *crosses and sits on the right arm of the sofa.* HENRY *sits in the easy chair* LC. ROGER *crosses to the fireplace.* VICTOR *is up* RC. JACKY *is up* LC.
ANNIE *enters up* C *and stands aside*)

ANNIE (*announcing*) Mrs Puffin.

(MRS PUFFIN *enters up* C)

MRS PUFFIN. 'Ullo, all. It's me again.

(ANNIE *exits up* C)

(*She moves* C) 'Ow are yer? I was getting frozen out there. What 'appened?

ETHEL. Ask Annie to remove the coffee things, someone, every cup and saucer.

MRS PUFFIN (*sitting* L *of Ethel on the sofa*) Don't worry, dearie, they're quite safe. If they was going for a Burton, I'd tell you. I was really sorry about your tea service. I was, really. Such a nice set, and I bet it was a good one, too. It's a funny thing—buy a cup and saucer in Woolworths and you 'ave 'em for years. But a good set—lummy, you've only got to look at 'em and they crack.

(JACKY *sits on the right arm of the easy chair* LC)

ETHEL. I had that tea service for years. Until you came.

MRS PUFFIN. Well, p'raps it was time you 'ad a new one. Always look on the bright side, I say. Now, if it was me . . .

ETHEL. Henry, will you please find out what she wants.

HENRY (*rising and moving* C) Yes, yes. Now, listen to me, Mrs Puffin. You must admit we have been very patient with you.

STEPHEN. Too damn patient.

HENRY. Exactly. Now, I want it to be firmly understood that the wedding between my daughter and Mr Parker will take place on Boxing Day as arranged. It was not our intention to see you . . .

MRS PUFFIN. Bit of a rumpus, eh? I thought I was out there a long time. I felt frozen. D'you know, I can 'ardly feel my poor old feet.

NICHOLAS (*crossing to the table up* L) Mrs Puffin, have a Deadly Nightshade. Warm the cockles of your heart. (*He pours a drink*)

MRS PUFFIN. If it gets down to my feet, I'll be 'appy. Thanks, love. (*To Henry*) You was saying?

HENRY. Mrs Puffin, have you had any more dreams?

MRS PUFFIN. Oh, I 'ad a lovely one a couple of nights ago. What Yul Brynner saw in me, I can't imagine. But when the alarm went off, 'e . . .

STEPHEN. Yul Brynner now. You see what I mean? Dammit, nobody's safe from her.

(NICHOLAS *hands the drink to Mrs Puffin then stands behind the sofa*)

MRS PUFFIN. Oh, it wasn't one of them sort of dreams. At least, I 'ope not. No, it couldn't be. Not in the middle of Piccadilly Circus.

HENRY. Did you dream about us?

MRS PUFFIN. No, dear, same old dream clicking along. But

bits keep on coming back. Oh, I know 'ow you feel. I do, really. But I can't 'elp it. I go about my daily work, when—click! Back a bit more comes.

STEPHEN. How many more clicks before we are safe from your ministrations?

MRS PUFFIN. Oh, no more. The final click came this morning. Just as I was telling young Seymour to wash 'is ears, and get off to school. If 'e can miss 'is ears, 'e will. "Look at the time", I say to him, " 'arf past eight", when—click! Click!

NICHOLAS. Click?

MRS PUFFIN. Click! Just like that, and I saw everything.

PAMELA (*rising*) What did you see, Mrs Puffin?

MRS PUFFIN (*looking at Pamela*) A lot, dear.

STEPHEN. A lot?

MRS PUFFIN. I think I can now safely say—*the* lot.

ETHEL. Well, for heaven's sake, tell us.

(MRS PUFFIN *sips her drink*)

MRS PUFFIN. Drop of good stuff, this. Got it in for Christmas?

JACKY. What happens, Mrs Puffin, what happens?

STEPHEN (*rising and moving* LC) Just a moment, Jacqueline. Mrs Puffin—everybody. I don't know what other extraordinary revelations this woman is going to concoct . . .

MRS PUFFIN. I 'aven't cockled anything. Everything I said would 'appen, 'as 'appened.

STEPHEN. On the contrary. Because the wedding is going to take place. So you are wrong. Second, if it didn't take place, and I say *if*, there would be a scandal, and I don't like scandals. The name Parker stands for something. No wedding, no partnership. I am sorry, Fordyce. You either listen to her or to me. (*He crosses to the easy chair down* L *and sits*)

HENRY. My dear Parker, of course we listen to you. Jacky and Victor will be happily married on Boxing Day. You see, Mrs Puffin, your clicks were wrong. Victor, you see how useless it has been having her in.

ETHEL. So there you are, Mrs Puffin.

HENRY. Exactly, my dear. Now, come along, Mrs Puffin, we want to play bridge.

(JACKY *rises and makes* HENRY *sit in the easy chair* LC)

JACKY. Just a minute. We have had Mrs Puffin in, and I think we ought to hear what she has to say. Do you agree, Victor?

VICTOR. Most certainly.

(PAMELA *sits on the right arm of the sofa*)

MRS PUFFIN. You've got to admit one thing—(*she nods to Ethel*) particularly you—I've been right up to now—your tea

service—(*to Stephen*) your despatch case with the wrong papers. About this bloke coming over water.
HENRY. On small details—yes. But only on small ones.
MRS PUFFIN (*to Stephen*) There's been a 'ell of a lot of small ones.
STEPHEN. Oh, very well—yes. Get on with it.
MRS PUFFIN. Good.
JACKY. What happens now?
MRS PUFFIN. Eight thirty. Zero hour. Someone's going to speak and shake the lot of yer. (*She rises, moves* C, *peers at the clock, then resumes her seat*) And it's just on eight thirty now.

(*There is a quick consulting of watches, then the others look at each other*)

STEPHEN. Well—who is it? Who is it? It's not me.
JACKY (*looking at Roger*) It's not me, either.
ETHEL. Well, it certainly isn't me. Is it you, Henry?
HENRY. No, it isn't. And it isn't you, Nicholas?
NICHOLAS. I know it isn't me. I know—it's Roger.
ALL (*ad lib*) Roger!
ROGER. No, no!
VICTOR (*moving* C *and vigorously polishing his glasses*) No, it's me.
JACKY. What—what—were you going to say, Victor?
MRS PUFFIN. I know.
VICTOR. Yes, you do, don't you?
STEPHEN. Well, we don't.
VICTOR. I'll get to the point quickly. As far as I'm concerned, the wedding between Jacky and me is—off.

(*There is a silence, then a general babble of voices*)

STEPHEN ⎫   ⎧ What!
HENRY   ⎬ (*together*)   ⎨ Now, look here, Victor . . .
ETHEL   ⎭   ⎩ Victor, how could you . . . ?
VICTOR (*raising his voice*) Please! Please!

(*Everyone quietens down.* NICHOLAS *sits on the back of the sofa*)

Actually, this is really just between the two of us, but as everyone, including Mrs Puffin, is affected, I'll speak openly. Do you mind, Jacky?
JACKY. No, Victor, I don't mind.
VICTOR (*directly to Jacky; very quietly*) We met two years ago, Jacky, didn't we? Our fathers met in business, the families became acquainted, we fell in love and got engaged. Just like that. Everything was fine at first, I mean, it still is, really—in a different sort of way. But we are not suited. I'm rather a dull chap, really, and Jacky—well, you're just Jacky. While I was wondering what to do, this new branch opening in Paris came up, and the wedding was put forward six months, and we were

getting married all of a sudden. Everything seemed to pile up on us. It was a bit difficult, Jacky, particularly as this partnership came into it, but the important thing was—I thought you loved me, and—hurting people doesn't come very easy.

JACKY. No, Victor, it doesn't.

VICTOR. There was another reason, too, but I could not hurt you, Jacky, and our parents were a bit over-powering, weren't they? Then, three days ago I met Mrs Puffin here. I heard what she said, and I really was impressed. Most impressed. If you remember, your father asked me outright if I loved you, and there you were looking at me, and I just couldn't say "no". Then Roger turned up, just as predicted. Since then you have been different. I mean, you have been just as sweet, if you understand me. Then yesterday I invited Roger for lunch in the City, and you as well. I saw the way you looked at each other. It was nice of you to try and hide it—you, too, Roger—but you can't hide things like that. So I left you together for the afternoon.

STEPHEN (*rising*) Good God!

VICTOR (*ignoring Stephen*) Mrs Puffin was right, wasn't she? You have been swept off your feet. You are in love with him?

JACKY. Yes, Victor, I am.

VICTOR (*lifting Jacky's left hand*) Keep the ring—for luck, Jacky.

(JACKY *suddenly kisses Victor then runs to* ROGER, *who embraces her*)

MRS PUFFIN. Ah! Love 'im!

ROGER. Victor, I don't know what to say.

STEPHEN. Dammit, I do! Now, look here, Victor . . .

NICHOLAS. Good for you, Victor. Good show, old boy. Jacky, congratulations. You, too, Roger.

PAMELA. Oh, Jacky—I hope you will both be very happy.

ETHEL. Jilted! Jilted! Just on the eve of her wedding.

NICHOLAS. It's not on the eve.

ETHEL. Don't argue. What about the presents?

NICHOLAS. I'll take Aunt Maud's pot back.

ETHEL. Henry, say something. Do you realize what has happened?

HENRY. Now, look here, Stephen, my daughter has been jilted just before her wedding . . .

STEPHEN. Jilted! Dammit, she's fallen in love with another man. Just before her wedding to my son. Fallen in love with an American.

ROGER. What's wrong with that?

STEPHEN. This will be a fine scandal. Scandal? Scandal! Get your hat and coat, Victor—we're going. (*He moves up* C, *then returns to* R *of Henry*) And, Fordyce, forget that partnership, it's off. *Off!*

Mrs Puffin. It ain't.
Stephen. What the devil do you mean?
Mrs Puffin. What I said—it ain't.
Stephen. Well, that's where you *are* wrong. It is. And Victor and I are getting out of here just as quick as we can. (*To Henry*) You received a Christmas card this morning from me, Fordyce, wishing you a Merry Christmas.
Henry. Er—yes, very kind of you.
Stephen. Cancel it. (*He moves up* C)

(Pamela *rises and moves up* RC)

Roger. Mr Parker, I feel kind of guilty about all this . . .
Stephen. Guilty! You feel guilty? (*He moves to Roger*) Let me tell you that I—
Mrs Puffin (*loudly*) Oi!
Stephen. —consider you the main cause of this . . .
Mrs Puffin (*louder*) *Oi!*
Stephen. Are you addressing me, madam?
Mrs Puffin. Yes, I am. (*She jerks a laconic thumb at Victor*) 'E ain't finished yet.
Stephen. Not finished? Good God! Hasn't he said enough?
Mrs Puffin. No, not by a long chalk. You all want to pin your ears back and get this little lot.
Stephen. If you say another word, Victor, I'll disown you.
Mrs Puffin. Don't talk daft! You won't.
Nicholas. That's telling him.
Mrs Puffin (*to Victor*) You carry on, love.
Victor. Thank you, Mrs Puffin, I will. This bit isn't easy.
Mrs Puffin. No—well, we know. Carry on, love.
Victor (*crossing down* R *and polishing his glasses*) Well, there is another reason why I did not feel quite the same way about Jacky.

(*There is a pause*)

Jacky. What is it, Victor?
Victor. Well—I'd—well, I'd fallen in love with somebody else.
Henry. He's a Mormon! That's what he is. (*He rises and moves* C) He finds helpless females, charms them, then casts them aside.
Jacky. Don't be silly, Father. I wasn't cast aside. I felt the same way as Victor, only I did not have the pluck to say so.
Ethel (*weeping*) Left at the altar. The disgrace of it. What are we going to do with the presents?
Mrs Puffin. Well, now's your chance to keep back a nice tea service. I should.
Ethel (*to Victor*) If you have fallen in love with some other girl, why don't you go to her?

HENRY. After the trouble you have let us in for, I'm sure the girl and her parents are welcome to you—(*to Stephen*) and your father.
JACKY. I think the girl will be very lucky. Good luck, Victor.
ROGER. That goes for me, too.
ETHEL. It's easy for you two. You will just be off to America. But what about us? We have to stay here and face the scandal.
NICHOLAS. There's no need. You can pop down to Bournemouth and take Aunt Maud's pot back. (*He rises and moves to Victor*) Good luck, old boy. Who is she?
VICTOR. It's a bit difficult, really.
NICHOLAS (*sagely*) Parent trouble?
VICTOR. Yes.
NICHOLAS. Hers or yours?
VICTOR. Er—both.
NICHOLAS. What does the girl say?
VICTOR. She doesn't know.
NICHOLAS. Do her parents?
VICTOR. No.
STEPHEN. And neither do I, and it's about time I did.
NICHOLAS. Take my advice, old boy, and tell the girl. Who is she?
VICTOR. Well—well—it's Pamela.

(*All eyes that have been on* VICTOR *suddenly switch to* PAMELA, *who just gazes at Victor*)

MRS PUFFIN. There!
HENRY (*moving down* C) What! Who did you say?
VICTOR. Pamela.
NICHOLAS. Good for you, Victor. Pam, what do you say?
PAMELA (*crossing slowly to Victor*) I—I—don't know what to say.
VICTOR. I'm sorry, Pamela. I never meant it to be like this. (*He looks around*) No, not like that. But you see how—how . . .
NICHOLAS. It's not very romantic, is it?
PAMELA (*breathlessly and obviously delighted*) It isn't really. (*She flings her arms around Victor*)
HENRY (*with a step towards Stephen*) Yes, but look here, he's already got one.
NICHOLAS. Shut up, Father, and sit down.

(HENRY *sits in the easy chair* LC)

(*He takes* PAMELA *and* VICTOR *by the hands and practically drags them to the door down* R) Now, look here, you two, pop in there and do your courting, you've got to make up for a lot of time. Try a little American technique, old boy. (*He removes Victor's glasses. To Pamela*) Leave everything to me.

(PAMELA *and* VICTOR *exit down* R.
NICHOLAS *closes the door*)

JACKY. That's wonderful! Oh, Roger, isn't it wonderful?
ROGER. It sure is. Good old Victor.

(*A babel breaks out from the parents*)

STEPHEN ⎫
HENRY ⎬ (*together*) ⎧ I don't agree.
ETHEL ⎭ ⎨ Now, look here, Parker ....
⎩ To think that all this time ...

NICHOLAS (*crossing to* C) Quiet!
MRS PUFFIN. Oi, oi, oi, oi!

(*The babel continues*)

(*She shouts*) *Oi!*

(*There is silence. The others look at Mrs Puffin*)

'E wants to say something.
NICHOLAS. Thank you.
MRS PUFFIN. That's better. Let's 'ave a little collaboration. Now, suppose you stop arguing and give youth a chance.
NICHOLAS. Thank you. On my right are two supremely happy people. (*He bows to Roger and Jacky*)
JACKY ⎫ (*together; with enthusiasm and vigorously applauding*)
ROGER ⎭ Hear, hear!
NICHOLAS. In the study are two more supremely happy people. (*To Mrs Puffin*) Am I right?
MRS PUFFIN. Not 'arf!
NICHOLAS. Mrs Puffin says "Not arf"! and she should know. In fact it is entirely due to that good lady that such a happy state of affairs exists. (*He leans over the left arm of the sofa*) Mrs Puffin, I think you're wonderful.
MRS PUFFIN. No, no, it just 'appens.
NICHOLAS. Mrs Puffin, I love you. What a pity there is a Mr Puffin.
STEPHEN. Now, listen to me, Nicholas ...
NICHOLAS. I hoped you were listening to me. But never mind, because at this moment we are going to listen to Mrs Puffin. Come on, my old darling, what happens now? Any more clicks?
MRS PUFFIN. No, I've clicked myself to a standstill. Well, there's nothing left to click about, is there. The two young couples get 'appily married and this 'ere partnership is definitely on. Well, look at your American angle, Mr Parker. (*To Roger*) I bet you're just bursting to work for Parker and Fordyce, ain't you?
ROGER. You bet I am.
MRS PUFFIN (*to Henry and Stephen*) It's a pity you two didn't 'ave a few more kids—then you could 'ave opened branches all

over the world. Blimey, it don't bear thinking of. Still, it's too late now. (*To the room in general*) I bet the only thing that gets steamed up about them two these days is their glasses. Anyway—at the end of my dream you are all good friends and open up the drinks. So what about it?

NICHOLAS (*crossing to the door down* R) What about those two in there?

(STEPHEN *moves down* L)

MRS PUFFIN. Oh, they're all right.

(NICHOLAS *opens the door, puts his head in and quickly withdraws it, closing the door behind him*)

NICHOLAS. Right again, Mrs Puffin. They're certainly making up for lost time. (*He opens the door and calls*) Here, you two, come on out. You've had long enough. (*He crosses to* C) Now, Father—Mr Parker—what about you two?

(PAMELA *and* VICTOR *enter down* R)

HENRY (*rising and moving to Stephen*) Well, Parker, old man . . .
STEPHEN. Listen, Henry, I think . . .
JACKY (*moving between Henry and Stephen*) Come on, darlings, don't dither.
HENRY. Well, Stephen, old chap . . .
STEPHEN. Henry, old man . . .

(HENRY *and* STEPHEN *shake hands.* NICHOLAS *crosses to the table up* L)

ROGER (*crossing to* C) Gee, that's swell!

(JACKY *kisses Stephen and Henry*)

ETHEL (*to Roger*) Oh, I am glad! You know, Roger, the first time I saw you I said, "What a nice young man".
ROGER. Thank you—Mother.
ETHEL (*delighted*) "Mother"! Well!
HENRY. Well, Roger . . .
STEPHEN. Dammit, man, congratulate him. He's got a damn fine girl, and so has my son.
ROGER. Thank you, sir. That's real swell of you.
HENRY (*moving to Roger*) I'm delighted, Roger. (*He shakes hands with Roger*)
JACKY. Come on, Nick, where are the drinks?
ROGER (*moving to Nicholas*) Here, I'll help you.

(NICHOLAS *and* ROGER *pour drinks*)

MRS PUFFIN. Yes, come on, Nicholas—the ridiculous—where's the drinks?

(JACKY *runs to Mrs Puffin and kisses her*)

JACKY. Dear Mrs Puffin, you are wonderful.
MRS PUFFIN. My old man ought to 'ear you say that.
NICHOLAS (*handing Mrs Puffin a drink*) There you are, my old darling, knock that back.

(ROGER *takes drinks to Henry and Stephen, returns for Jacky's and his own and stands above the easy chair* LC. NICHOLAS *takes a tray of drinks to Ethel, Pamela and Victor, then takes a drink for himself and stands up* R. JACKY *joins Roger*)

ROGER (*to Mrs Puffin*) You're great, and before we go back to the States we've got to see a lot of you.
MRS PUFFIN. That's a nice change. I was beginning to think I'd worn me welcome out. (*She drinks*)
HENRY (*crossing to* c) Now, everyone, a toast!
MRS PUFFIN. A toast? Lummy! You never said nothing about a toast. I've drunk mine.
NICHOLAS (*crossing to the table up* L) Mrs Puffin, you shall have some more. (*He grabs the shaker and refills Mrs Puffin's glass*)
MRS PUFFIN. Thanks, love. I should 'ate to be left out of a toast.
HENRY. You don't want a speech from me . . .
ALL. Hear, hear!
MRS PUFFIN. I do.
HENRY. Thank you, Mrs Puffin. You know, I shall have to make one at the reception, and I don't want to make the same speech twice. I probably shall, because then, as now, I will just ask you all to raise your glasses to the happy couples, Roger and Jacky, Victor and Pamela. Long life and happiness.
ALL. Long life and happiness.
MRS PUFFIN. Well, down the little red lane. (*She downs her drink in one*)
ETHEL. Do you know, I feel quite excited.
HENRY. Well, you're not the only one, dear.
NICHOLAS. Mother, I believe you're tiddly.
ETHEL. Nicholas! I'm not.
NICHOLAS. Then you should be. This is a celebration. (*He holds out the shaker*) Let's have a party. Mrs Puffin, another drink. You get tiddly, too. Or are you? (*He withdraws the shaker*)
MRS PUFFIN. I could be, ducks. You want to coax me? (*She holds out her glass*)
NICHOLAS. Yes, my old darling, then you can go home and dream of me.
HENRY. Mrs Puffin, how far did you get in your dream?
MRS PUFFIN (*pointing to Roger*) Directly 'e came into the room, and your daughter, the pretty dear, she came straight to 'im— like a bird from a cage. Well—it 'ad to 'appen, 'cos otherwise, why did I dream it?

JACKY. But if you woke up then, what about tonight? Was that another dream?
MRS PUFFIN. I don't want to say. Tonight's another story.
HENRY. Why?
MRS PUFFIN (*pointing to Victor*) 'E came round to my 'ouse this afternoon.
STEPHEN. Who came round where?
MRS PUFFIN. Your son came round to my 'ouse.

(*There is general reaction*)

STEPHEN. What?
VICTOR. Oh, dear, I was going to tell you . . .
PAMELA. Victor, do you mean . . .?
VICTOR. It took me nearly twenty-four hours to trace Mrs Puffin. I called there this afternoon.
HENRY. That's how she knew we'd all be here tonight.
MRS PUFFIN. All I knew was, I had to get here just before eight-thirty. 'Is nibs told me roughly what he was going to say and after that I 'ad to plug the partnership and everything. I 'ope I played my part well.
JACKY. Mrs Puffin, you old fraud!
MRS PUFFIN. Only about tonight, love, the rest was genuine.
VICTOR. So was tonight genuine for me.
STEPHEN. Do you mean to tell me that tonight was engineered?
MRS PUFFIN. In a manner of speaking—yes.
VICTOR. Yes. You see, I knew Mrs Puffin was right, and I knew I was right, and I wanted to find out whether Pam felt the same, and I wanted to help Jacky and Roger . . .
PAMELA (*flinging her arms around Victor*) Victor, darling, you are wonderful!
NICHOLAS (*suddenly roaring with laughter*) Victor, I never knew you had it in you.
STEPHEN (*laughing*) Neither did I.

(*The others join in the laughter*)

NICHOLAS. Well, I think a few words from the visiting fireman wouldn't be out of place. Mrs Puffin, the floor is yours.
MRS PUFFIN. My Gawd! What for?
NICHOLAS. A speech, me old darling.
MRS PUFFIN. A speech. (*She rises and staggers* C) I 'aven't made a speech since my wedding day, when I said, "I will, I do, I will", and 'ave done ever since. (*She finishes her drink*) Where are my gloves? (*She puts her glass on the coffee-table*) Oh, I've got 'em on. Do you know, I believed I'm sloshed.

(*There is general laughter.* ETHEL *rises and moves down* R)

ALL. Good night, Mrs Puffin.
HENRY. Good night, Mrs Puffin—and pleasant dreams.

STEPHEN. But not about us.

MRS PUFFIN. No fear. I've given up 'aving cheese for my supper in case I see your fizz-ogg. But I did 'ave another dream last night. I'm just off to Number Ten Downing Street.

QUICK CURTAIN

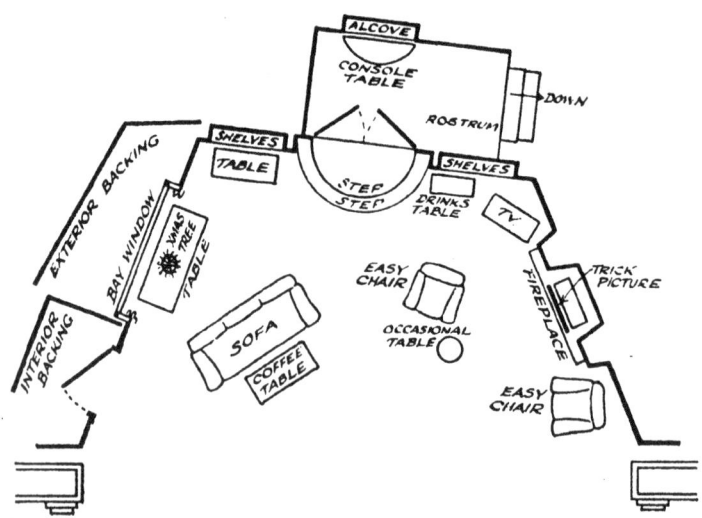

FURNITURE AND PROPERTY LIST

ACT I

On stage—On wall above and below door L : miniatures
    Table (in window bay) *On it* : decorated Christmas tree with fairy
        lights, box with cigarettes, table lighter, ashtray, ornamental
        Christmas candle, Christmas cards
    Window curtains and pelmet
    Table (up R) *On it:* large table-lamp, telephone with long flex,
        silver basket with five oranges
    Shelves (up R) *On them:* ornaments, floral decoration, Christmas
        cards, books
    Shelves (up L) *On them:* ornaments, floral decoration, Christmas
        cards, tantalus with sherry, whisky and port, bottle of gin,
        syphon of soda, cocktail jug, lighter
    Table (up L) *On it:* tray with 7 cocktail glasses, 3 whisky glasses
    Television set. *On it:* table-lamp, ashtray, Christmas cards
    On mantelpiece: box with cigarettes, lighter, ashtray, ornate gilt clock
        set at 4.30, pair of candlesticks with candles, Christmas
        cards
    Over mantelpiece: picture in heavy frame, 2 electric wall-brackets, 2
        miniatures
    Basket fire grate
    Fender
    Hearth rug
    In grate: broken pieces of Doulton cup
    On wall down L: picture with decoration
    Sofa. *On it:* cushions
    Easy chair down L: *On it:* cushion
    Easy chair LC: *On it:* cushion
    Occasional table (LC) *On it:* pencil and pad
    Coffee-table (RC) *On it:* 12 letters, paper knife
    Carpet on floor
    In hall: console table. *On it:* bowl of flowers, electric wall bracket
        with decoration
    Light switches R of double doors
Double doors open
Window curtains open
Door down R closed
Fire on
Light fittings off

Off stage—6 parcels (PAMELA)
    5 parcels (JACKY)
    Silver tray. *On it:* cloth, 4 cups, 5 saucers, 5 teaspoons, prepared
        breakable cup, 5 plates, plate of biscuits, jug of milk, basin of
        sugar with tongs (ANNIE)
    Shopping bag. *In it:* celery (MRS PUFFIN)
    Cup and saucer and spoon (ANNIE)
    Silver salver. *On it:* telegram (ANNIE)

Personal—PAMELA: handbag
    JACKY: handbag
    MRS PUFFIN: handbag. *In it:* purse, handkerchief
    HENRY: wallet. *In it:* ten one-pound notes

ACT II

Strike—Broken crockery
       Telegram
       Parcel
       Picture from fireplace
       Paper-knife and letters from coffee-table

Set—On table up R: Ethel's bag. *In it:* smelling salts. Clock on mantelpiece to 8.15
Double doors open
Window curtains closed
Door down R closed
Hall bracket on
Other fittings off
Fire on
Christmas tree lights on

Off stage—Tray. *On it:* coffee for five (ANNIE)
        Sheaf of papers (ETHEL)
        Despatch case. *In it:* envelope with papers (STEPHEN)

Personal—ETHEL: handkerchief
        VICTOR: glasses, handkerchief

ACT III

Strike—Coffee things
       Dirty glasses
       Ethel's bag
       Despatch case and papers
       Tidy room generally

Set—Additional Christmas cards
       Holly wreath over mantelpiece in place of picture
       15 cocktail glasses on table up L
       Cocktail jug and spoon on table up L
       Set clock to 7.30
Double doors open
Window curtains closed
Door down R closed
Hall bracket on
Table-lamps on
Wall-brackets off
Fire on
Christmas tree lights on

Off stage—Tray. *On it:* coffee for 8 (ANNIE)

Personal—VICTOR: glasses, handkerchief, watch

LIGHTING PLOT

Property fittings required—3 wall-brackets, 2 table-lamps, fire, fairy lights for Christmas tree

Interior. A drawing-room. The same scene throughout

THE APPARENT SOURCES OF LIGHT ARE—in daytime, a large window R and at night, wall-brackets over the fireplace L and in the hall up C, and table-lamps up R and up L.

THE MAIN ACTING AREAS—cover the whole stage

ACT I   A Winter afternoon

To open: Effect of dull daylight
            Fire on
            Fittings off

No cues

ACT II   Evening

To open: The room in darkness
            Fire on
            Christmas tree lights, on
            Hall bracket, on
            Other fittings off
            Dark outside window

Cue 1	ETHEL switches on lights *Snap in wall-brackets L* *Snap in covering lights*	(page 25)
Cue 2	PAMELA switches on lamp up R *Snap in lamp up R* *Snap in covering lights*	(page 25)
Cue 3	JACKY switches on lamp up L *Snap in lamp up L* *Snap in covering lights*	(page 25)

ACT III   Evening

To open: Table-lamp up L, on
            Table-lamp up R, on
            Hall bracket, on
            Fire, on
            Christmas tree lights, on

Cue 4	ROGER switches on wall-brackets *Snap in wall-brackets* *Snap in covering lights*	(page 51)
Cue 5	VICTOR exits up C *Dim all lights to* BLACK-OUT *for fifteen seconds*	(page 56)

EFFECTS PLOT

ACT I

Cue 1	PAMELA: "... end of August" *Front door bell rings*	(page 4)
Cue 2	ETHEL: "I mean her" *Front door bell rings*	(page 9)
Cue 3	ETHEL: "... you for calling" *Front door slams*	(page 11)
Cue 4	MRS PUFFIN: "Well, I'm off" *Crash of crockery*	(page 17)
Cue 5	HENRY: "... thing is impossible" *Front door bell rings*	(page 19)
Cue 6	MRS PUFFIN: "... a talk with you" *Telephone rings*	(page 22)
Cue 7	HENRY: "Good night, Mrs Puffin" *Picture falls*	(page 24)

ACT II

Cue 8	HENRY: "... deeds of partnership" *Front door bell rings*	(page 28)
Cue 9	HENRY: "... time for levity" *Front door bell rings*	(page 29)
Cue 10	MRS PUFFIN: "... 'appened that way" *Front door bell rings*	(page 34)
Cue 11	HENRY: "—very messy" *Telephone rings*	(page 38)
Cue 12	HENRY: "... ever had them" *Carol singers sing "Good King Wenceslas"*	(page 43)
Cue 13	HENRY (off) "Go away." *Singing ceases abruptly*	(page 44)

ACT III

Cue 14	ROGER and JACKY embrace *Door slam*	(page 49)
Cue 15	JACKY: "Nicky mixed these" *Front door bell rings*	(page 51)
Cue 16	NICHOLAS: "... all the Forces" *Front door bell rings*	(page 54)
Cue 17	ETHEL: "... going to play ..." *Front door bell rings*	(page 59)

www.ingramcontent.com/pod-product-compliance
Ingram Content Group UK Ltd.
Pitfield, Milton Keynes, MK11 3LW, UK
UKHW021845210426
5322IPUK00022B/478